CW01084200

Leading Strategy Execution

*How to engage employees
and implement your strategies*

Christine Antunes : Christophe Korda

Philippe Korda : Suresh Mistry

KoganPage

LONDON PHILADELPHIA NEW DELHI

Publisher's note

Every possible effort has been made to ensure that the information contained in this book is accurate at the time of going to press, and the publishers and authors cannot accept responsibility for any errors or omissions, however caused. No responsibility for loss or damage occasioned to any person acting, or refraining from action, as a result of the material in this publication can be accepted by the editor, the publisher or any of the authors.

First published in Great Britain and the United States in 2010 by Kogan Page Limited

120 Pentonville Road	525 South 4th Street, #241	4737/23 Ansari Road
London N1 9JN	Philadelphia PA 19147	Daryaganj
United Kingdom	USA	New Delhi 110002
www.koganpage.com		India

All cartoons by Barros, 2010

ISBN   978 0 7494 6056 3
E-ISBN   978 0 7494 6064 8

British Library Cataloguing-in-Publication Data

A CIP record for this book is available from the British Library.

Library of Congress Cataloging-in-Publication Data

Leading strategy execution : how to engage employees and implement your strategies / Suresh Mistry ... [et al.]. – 1st ed.
      p. cm.
   Includes bibliographical references.
   ISBN 978-0-7494-6056-3 – ISBN 978-0-7494-6064-8 1. Employee motivation. 2. Management–Employee participation. 3. Leadership. I. Mistry, Suresh.
   HF5549.5.M63L423 2010
   658.3'14–dc22

                                        2009048752

Typeset by Saxon Graphics Ltd, Derby
Printed and bound in India by Replika Press Pvt Ltd

Contents

Acknowledgements

Thanks are due to our clients, without whom most of these pages would be blank. Indeed, our writing is the fruit of experience that we have accumulated from them over years in the training and management consultancy sectors. With the help of our consultants, we have assisted some remarkable companies, very often household names known on every continent and in every business sector.

We would also like to thank our staff and colleagues at Korda & Partners. Every day, all over the world, they help to enrich our experience and to hone, refine and simplify our approach.

Thanks go to Anthony Withers and his team at Anglia Translations and to Yves Barros, whose hilarious cartoons perfectly complement the serious lessons in the book.

We owe a considerable debt of gratitude to our colleague Laura Kosinski, whose indefatigable research has ensured that no major aspect of the subject has been overlooked.

Lastly, thank *you*, reader, for having the courage to open this book (and not just look at the pictures). In our eyes this simple act already places you among the most open, cultured and proactive of people. Reading the rest of the book and putting our recommendations into practice will be child's play for you!

Introduction

Giving our organizations the extra energy they need

At one time or another, we have all struggled to take regular exercise, to stop smoking, to adopt a healthy diet or to learn a new skill, despite our best intentions. For an organization it is infinitely harder – because decisions taken by certain people have to be put into practice by others. Within a large corporation, this may involve hundreds, thousands or even hundreds of thousands of people, spread over numerous sites in many different countries, separated by linguistic and cultural barriers as much as by time zones, mountains and oceans. How can you ensure that all those people implement the same strategy intelligently, harmoniously, vigorously and – if possible – enthusiastically?

Many writers have already addressed the issue of strategy implementation.

Some books rely upon the balanced scorecard concept, which involves breaking a central objective down into a series of indicators at every level of an organization. Such books are useful. Yet, in practice, do the problems that we face really stem from a lack of indicators? Is that the main problem? Within the companies that we are familiar with, the general feeling is rather more that there is too much information and a lack of meaning.

Other books explain different approaches to change management. Once again, they make for a sensible and useful read, having the merit of arguing that more account should be taken of the human dimension within organizations. Unfortunately, those works provide (often complex) analytical tools rather than truly practical solutions.

Thus, in addressing this complex subject, we wanted to write a simple, specific operational book, a book that addresses real problems and offers workable solutions. Firstly, it is for senior executives, who are leading strategy implementation. Secondly, it is for business and project managers, who must both apply company decisions and promote their own initiatives, sometimes without access to direct hierarchical authority. Lastly, it is for anyone, whatever their role, who wants to see progress, to see strategies put into effect, to see action plans implemented and projects brought to fruition.

To sum up, this book is intended as a practical guide. This means that you must start reading it with a specific objective in mind: if you don't, no solution will grab your attention.

We have built this book around a single central idea: what habitually holds back the implementation of strategies within our companies is not a lack of resources, intelligence or goodwill. It is our inability to give our organizations the extra energy they need to bring projects to fruition. Indeed, within a company, the entire corporate mass is already fully occupied (sometimes to saturation point) in dealing with a multitude of everyday problems and a range of ongoing projects. If you want a strategic decision to be implemented, you will need to find some extra human energy.

Unlike time, the amount of individual or collective energy at our disposal within a day is not predetermined. We all sometimes feel exhausted when we have done almost nothing. In contrast, we can also feel full of energy after having completed a string of tasks. Unlike money, the energy that we transmit to others does not impoverish us and the energy that we expend can be renewed indefinitely. Unlike material goods, energy cannot be stored. We must create positive stress within our organizations on a daily basis.

In *The Power of Full Engagement,* Jim Loehr and Tony Schwartz correctly point out that 'leaders inspire or demoralize others through the way in which they mobilize, focus, invest and renew the collective energy of those they lead'.[1] Remarkably, their book deals with energy management from an individual viewpoint, including drawing on the example of top sportspeople. For our part, we offer a method designed to provide an organization with the extra energy needed to implement a strategic initiative.

Structurally, this book comprises three parts, which it is probably useful to read in order.

Part 1 is entitled 'The energy of engagement: Wouldn't life be easier if people wanted to do what you expect of them?' Indeed, the first question to ask yourself concerns the energy of engagement: do the people around you want to commit themselves to action? For that, your message must be delivered, heard, understood, accepted – and it must generate enthusiasm. In Chapters 1 to 5, we help you to identify where your problem is located and how to achieve significant progress in these different areas.

Part 2 is entitled 'The energy of change: Wouldn't it be so much easier if they changed their habits?' Indeed, it is often the case that people have a sincere desire to contribute to an initiative, but do not really know how to go about it. This may be due to an ingrained company culture, a lack of training or an inability to replicate the best practices that they see around them. So, in Chapters 6 to 8, we seek to explain how to change company culture more quickly, how to introduce more economical and more productive training initiatives and how to spread successful practices throughout an organization.

Part 3, the final part, is entitled 'The energy of management: What if your middle managers actually served some purpose?' Of course, these days it is standard practice to denigrate middle management:

they are often deemed to create inertia and financial waste within modern organizations. On the contrary, experience has convinced us that middle managers play an absolutely irreplaceable role in getting a company going. However, they do still need specific assistance to ensure that they promote decisions, address the real priorities, pursue inspiring objectives and develop a 'performance ethic'. In Chapters 9 to 12, we offer practical solutions designed to achieve this.

Throughout this book, each chapter begins by presenting a real scenario that will help you to relate our advice to situations similar to those that you may encounter.[2]

Lastly, in order to help you to use this book effectively, at the end of each chapter we present a series of specific questions for you to ask yourself about the specific circumstances of concern to you. On each occasion, you will even be invited to hand the book to another person and to answer aloud the questions that they read out. Do not skip these few questions, as it is from your own answers that you will learn some of the most important lessons in this book.

We hope that you enjoy reading it!

Notes

1. Jim Loehr and Tony Schwartz (2003) *The Power of Full Engagement*, Free Press, New York.
2. Forenames have been changed and surnames have not been quoted. In certain cases, the business sector has been changed slightly in order to prevent the identification of companies or individuals.

Part 1
The energy of engagement

Wouldn't life be easier if people wanted
to do what you expect of them?

A major corporation is adopting a new strategy based on the quest for top-quality customer service. It launches an ambitious project, 'Quality First', with the aim of ensuring all personnel focus on this priority. Six months after the launch, a staff survey is carried out. Some of the interview scripts sent to head office by the research institute responsible grab the attention of senior executives.

Firstly, there are those revealing a profound ignorance of the project: 'I don't know what you're talking about, to be honest'; 'Quality First? I'm sure that I've seen that slogan... it must be an advertising campaign for customers'; 'Yes, I know what it is, but I'm not involved because I work at head office'; 'Yes, but they haven't talked about it to front-line staff like us – I reckon that it's more a head office project.'

There are also those comments that demonstrate great scepticism: 'Yeah, Quality First, that's the official corporate position, but the truth is that for top management it's all about profits.' 'That's all very well, but we don't get the resources to provide real quality.' 'Slogans and bosses come and go, you know, but we just carry on as before.'

Lastly, there are those comments that indicate some support in principle, but without this engendering any action in practice: 'I don't plan to do anything myself, but I think that the project is a step in the right direction'; 'We'll see where it leads, but it certainly can't do us any harm'; 'It's a great idea in itself, but the new indicators mean that our bosses are even more stressed out than before, so we let them worry about it and carry on as usual.'

Whatever the relevance of the Quality First project and whatever the abilities of those who designed it, it currently has almost zero chance of yielding any positive results for the customer. The energy of engagement is missing. Five red lights stand in its way.

Firstly, the message from top management has not reached all those people responsible for converting it into new priorities, new methods and new behaviour. Secondly, where the message has been delivered it has not always been heard. Where it has been heard, it has not always been understood... and, where it has been understood, it has not always been accepted. Lastly, even when it has been accepted, it has not generated enthusiasm for action.

The first part of this book will help us to turn those five red lights to green. Chapter 1 is entitled 'Open the box of secrets' and addresses the difficulty that you may sometimes experience in conveying difficult messages to your people. 'Chapter 2, 'Capture everyone's attention', explains how to ensure that your key messages get through. Chapter 3, 'Spell it out in words of one syllable', offers you some tools to enable your plans and instructions to be better understood. 'Chapter 4, 'Mould opinion', explains how to ensure that your people show more commitment to your priorities. Lastly, Chapter 5, 'Provide an emotional spark', shows you how to turn that commitment into a desire to act.

1 Open the box of secrets

Perhaps it really would be worth talking to them about it...

A candle loses none of its light by lighting another candle.
Japanese proverb

Summary

Enter our 'energy of engagement' section and discover how to build commitment by providing inspirational communication. Learn what to include in communication to enable all your people to act and how to design the communication to appeal to different perspectives and values. Finally, find out how to ensure all your people are clear about their specific roles and what they must do now.

'There's an ill wind blowing, Carl. We need to make even more cutbacks. I hope that you have other clients.'

Carl rocks on his heels. He runs the New York office of an advertising agency and he could be just about to lose his principal client. Two-thirds of his people work on this account. For months now, Carl has been dreading this moment. He has been trying to get the whole agency behind an 'Everyone's a Salesperson' project so as to quickly pull in more business, but without great success to date.

Carl is anxious for two reasons. Firstly, he has developed very close ties with his client's opposite numbers: it hurts him to see them in turmoil when he is powerless to help. Secondly, he feels a close bond with the people at his agency. He feels responsible for their jobs and really wants to continue to offer them projects through which they can grow and develop.

When he gets back to the office, Carl is struck by the lively, happy atmosphere. Vigorous discussions are taking place, the phones are ringing and there's laughter everywhere. Not only has the agency racked up the best growth rates in the sector over the past three years, but Carl has also put together a real team here.

When he explains the situation to Tom, his finance director, his colleague interjects: 'I hope that you are going to talk about this at the team meeting tomorrow. They all need to understand that, if they don't get their fingers out, they are going to be out of a job.'

Carl is quick to respond: 'We can't preach doom and gloom. If we tell the whole truth, they will be completely demoralized. It would cause panic. We've already launched "Everyone's a Salesperson". They're a great bunch, so let's trust them to deliver. Success is just around the corner.'

Yet, deep inside, he is not convinced. Yes, the project has been launched, but old habits die hard. For a moment Carl closes his eyes and wonders in frustration: 'What on earth are they waiting for?'

Carl's problem is also your problem. It is a problem for each of us whenever we find it hard to admit that words are no substitute for action or whenever we find it difficult to get people to do what we want.

So why do intelligent people with responsible positions within an organization refuse to acknowledge the truth? Why do we remain silent or in denial when in reality we need to speak up loud and clear?

When the situation requires us to roll out an initiative within a company, we often ask ourselves the same questions: 'Should we come clean about everything?', 'Should we tell them everything about the project?' or even 'Do I need to tell them what we expect of them?' Later, when we look back, too often we find that no real progress has been made or that the progress has been too slow or too feeble. Despite universal support and the will to move forward, the habits of the past are deeply ingrained.

So, we sigh to ourselves, 'What on earth are they waiting for?' Well, in the first instance, the problem might simply be that we have not been totally up front about the situation, the project or our specific expectations.

Provide true inspiration... and explain the situation

Everyone knows that the search for meaning is a key motivational factor for individuals. You are probably prepared to tackle many difficult and demanding challenges in your life, provided that you know why you are doing it. That is why so many senior executives cite transparency and genuine communication among their key operating principles. It is a pity that so few of them seem to mean it. 'Tell them the truth'; 'Inform without excluding'; 'Never stop explaining and communicating': the intentions are always the same... So why do we often do the opposite?

From a practical viewpoint, there is no shortage of reasons. When it is an opportunity that lies behind a company initiative, communicating is a pleasure. 'This new market is just right for us.' 'This new technology offers us great prospects.' 'This acquisition will make us market leaders again.' So it is quite easy to explain, to reaffirm, to motivate and to inspire commitment. However, when the initiative is motivated by a problem, it is quite a different matter. 'We must take action because our profits are crumbling', '... because our competitors are overtaking us', '... because our customers are voting with their feet...': not a message to inspire people!

If Carl is hesitant about sharing vital information with his team, it is not out of a desire to conceal or to manipulate. He simply does not want to worry his people. Essentially, he wants to protect them.

It is true that spreading bad news can affect the morale of the troops. Some of our people may withdraw from the fray at the very moment when we need them most. Others, often our best people, may even think of deserting the sinking ship. This risk is particularly great in certain business sectors and certain occupations: those where good people are hard to find. So there is a real risk of further aggravating a difficult situation. Thus the fear of demoralization sometimes leads us to downplay problems. This risks making it more difficult to mobilize our teams to implement solutions. If we minimize a problem, no one will work 100 per cent to resolve it.

Another cause of hesitation is the risk that information will be leaked outside the company.

On a factory tour, the new CEO of an automotive group is waxing lyrical about his desire to produce quality cars: 'Even my own company car has broken down twice!' The message is received loud and clear by staff in attendance. Unfortunately, the next day several media organizations have picked up on this. The manufacturer seeks to deny it, but various employees confirm that they heard the CEO say just that. The company's brand image is badly dented.

It is true: raising a problem in front of staff involves taking a risk that it will become a subject for gossip with third parties – customers in particular. However, it is a risk worth taking: if a problem exists and we do not inform those capable of resolving it, then we are preventing them from providing a solution.

Sometimes, it is also the fear of being singled out that leads us to restrict the information flow. As a senior manager of six years' standing at a ready-to-wear clothing distributor, Laura had persistently resisted her people's arguments that they should grow online sales: 'That's not what we do.' Her direct competitors saw things differently and gained market share. Within two years, Laura's brand had lost ground. When she finally bit the bullet and authorized a vast online sales project, Laura baulked at spelling out the reasons for this decision. She explained that she did not wish to fuel pointless controversy within the company. She added that action was all that counted now. Yet deep down she was well aware that she felt uncomfortable with colleagues who might have accused her of a lack of vision in previous years.

Kings and queens rarely start revolutions. Similarly, for a manager who has been in post for some time, it requires considerable courage to inform staff that something is going badly wrong. However, if we do not have the courage to say what is going wrong, things will not get better.

In other cases, we may believe that a situation is complex and that our people are not really capable of understanding. This is particularly true where the workforce is made up of people who lack education or skills. 'Why confuse them by raising issues that they do not understand, when all that's needed is to tell them what to do?'

Yet every experiment carried out over recent decades has demonstrated that our people are much more capable of comprehending economic challenges than their senior managers believe – provided that management takes the time to explain the issues to them. If we trust our people to implement a solution, we must also accept that they are capable of understanding the problem.

Lastly, and this is what mostly happens, we may not inform people about the situation because we are convinced that 'they already know'. It is true that employees have access to a glut of information (television, radio, newspapers, internet, etc), so they probably are aware that their business sector is subject to centralization, new competitors, new low-cost suppliers, regulatory changes and shifts in customer demand. They have heard about it. They may even have heard a great deal about it. Yet there are thousands of different ways of interpreting information. Is this new information or does it merely confirm what they already knew? Is it of major or minor importance? Are we on the sidelines or directly affected? Is it a threat or an opportunity? So, depending upon different perceptions and upon messages received externally (media, family and friends), a collective opinion tends to develop in each little work group.[1] That collective opinion then becomes hard to shift.

Thus, even if we believe that the people around us 'already know', it is absolutely key that we should help them to interpret information. We must help our people to make connections between different types of information: if sales have fallen, it's because a competitor is cheaper, and we therefore need to improve our productivity. In short, the important thing is that not only should our people possess information, but crucially they should interpret it usefully and constructively.

As we have seen, there is no shortage of 'good reasons' to avoid talking to our people about problems that need to be resolved. So we all sometimes hold back certain information that we should be sharing.

We can also end up talking about the problem... but not enough about the plan.

Be direct: explain your plan

Jake is the operations manager for a mail order company. In order to combat cut-price competition from new entrants to the market, he has convinced the entire board to launch a major project designed to reduce delivery times from 48 hours to 24: 'This is the project that will put us ahead of the pack for at least five years,' he explains. He selects a 10-strong project team and tells them the details of the plan. All divisional managers are also informed at length and in detail.

Yet during the initial phases of the project, problems just mount up. Each change in a process or IT procedure arouses fierce resistance, as does every minor organizational change. On the ground, people raise objection after objection. 'It's hopeless,' says one project team member after another. Alone in his office, Jake looks again at the project presentation slides. 'But we didn't miss a trick,' he sighs.

No doubt Jake was right: his presentation was very comprehensive. The problem was that it greatly underestimated the number of people who would be affected by his project. It is a mistake anyone can make! In fact, when a company launches a major initiative, the project team and senior managers are usually bombarded with detailed information. Yet, too often, the majority of people who will be directly affected by a project are forgotten.

There are several reasons for this.

It may be that we do not appreciate the changes that the project will cause to the daily routine of our people. Alternatively, we may underestimate the importance of those changes to the people concerned: what might seem a mere detail to Jake may be a major component in the daily routine of many employees. More generally, managers often underestimate the number of people who may be affected by a strategic initiative. Naturally, there are the project leaders. There are those who must spread the word. Then there are those who have to push it through at various organizational levels. Yet there are also all those who must absorb it and understand it, if only to avoid holding things up. There may be a lot of people involved here. All the people – or groups – whose roles we underestimate will remind us of their importance sooner or later, if only through their inaction.

In other cases, it is a concern for competitive confidentiality that causes large numbers of people to be kept in the dark. It is true that, if Jake publicizes this 24-hour delivery project too widely (or too soon), he may unwittingly encourage his main competitors to copy it and steal a march. So you need to carefully judge the point at which project information should be shared with those who will contribute to its implementation. If the project has been well prepared, it will already be too late for competitors to respond. An obsession with secrecy may thwart your competitors, but it might also prevent your own people from taking action.

Sometimes, we also tend to believe that our people are already swamped by a flood of information. 'They have their work and their customers. It's our job to take care of the project.' However, as they have a role to play in implementing that strategic initiative, it is part of our job to find ways of sending out clear information as to what the project involves. An overload of information about minor details is no excuse for keeping people in the dark about major issues.

In short, therefore, it is not enough to show your people the 'why', but you must also show them the 'what'. Nevertheless, there is a risk that none of this will be of any use if the 'how' is not explained to them...

Spell it out: tell them exactly what they have to do

Cathy is a creative director at the advertising agency managed by Carl. She is extremely competent and highly motivated. She is proud of the agency's results, viewed as outstanding in the sector: strong growth, major clients and large, interesting projects. Furthermore, it is a happy office, and staff are fiercely committed and mutually supportive. However, for the past six months, Cathy has clearly sensed a shift in the mood. A while ago, Carl presented a project entitled 'Everyone's a Salesperson', designed to maintain and develop turnover in what is turning out to be a tricky period. Ever since, Cathy has been worried. At noon today, Carl arrived in the office looking troubled, which was unlike him. Now he is deep in conversation with Tom, the finance director, and their expressions do not augur well. Cathy watches them. She is afraid yet feels powerless. She would like to make herself more useful, but does not know how.

Too often, we just present our people with the context, the objectives sought and key priorities for action. Of course, all this is absolutely vital. Yet, a few months later, we look around and are astonished to see how little has been done: 'What on earth are they waiting for?'

We fondly imagine that each individual will spontaneously be able to make the connection between the general priorities that we have announced and their own work. Yet it is rarely that simple. As creative director, Cathy is unclear precisely how she can help the 'Everyone's a Salesperson' project to succeed. Although she does feel directly involved, she is unable to answer the following questions: 'Just what is changing for me?' and 'Exactly what is expected of me?' Whether you are a senior executive, a middle manager or a project leader, it is not enough to say what you want to do; you need to explain to all your people exactly what is expected of them.

In conclusion to this chapter...

You've got the message: in order to instil the energy of commitment, the crucial first step is to have the courage to open the box of secrets to explain to your people the nature of the situation, the project and the specific role that they must play.

Take this book and give it to your partner. Get them to ask you the following questions:

- You know that project you talk about every evening: have you 'truly inspired' the people involved and explained to them the reasons why it is so important to act decisively?

  - If there was a positive reason or opportunity that gave rise to the project, have you fully explained it?

  - If it was a problem or risk, have you overcome your fear of damaging the morale of the troops? The fear of information leaking outside the company? The fear of feeling that you personally are in the firing line?

- Have you placed sufficient trust in people and their ability to understand what is at stake?

- Have you taken account of the fact that, however much information people receive, they need help to interpret it constructively?

- Have you really 'opened the box of secrets' and explained the contents of your project?

- Have you presented your project to all those people capable of helping to implement it?

- Have you fully appreciated how a change that may be minor to you can be important to others?

- If your project is confidential for now, have you identified the point at which you will need to inform the people concerned?

- Have you provided your people with very clear information – since you tell me that they are already drowning in a flood of data?

- Have you 'spelt it out' and explained to people exactly what they have to do?

- Are you capable of putting into a few words exactly what you expect of each individual?

- Have you taken the time to explain this to them?

If your partner is unconvinced by your answers, you undoubtedly still have work to do. Otherwise, well done! You can move on to the next chapter.

Note

1. Read *Organisational Behaviour* by Stephen P Robbins *et al* (Pearson Education, Harlow, 2007).

2 Capture everyone's attention

Why they never know what's going on, although they have been fully informed

Information must belong to those people who need to know.
Lou Gerstner, former CEO, IBM

Summary

Let's now focus on how to engage your people and capture their attention. We'll explore the factors that connect your people to your strategy and how to make your messages stand out from the daily noise. In addition, discover the ways in which each one of us absorbs information and how you should tune into these 'wavelengths' to increase the impact of your communication.

The meeting has just begun. Arriving from head office on the morning train, Kate has come to quiz a group of front-line staff. The subject? Implementing the 'Innovate for Change' initiative that she has been leading for the past year at this major public corporation.

As soon as the initial brainstorming session begins, Kate is worried. None of the participants has understood the purpose of the meeting, because none of them has even heard of 'Innovate for Change'. Kate struggles to conceal her irritation. How can this be possible after a year? She is absolutely convinced of the benefits that this initiative offers the company – and its staff, above all. Better working conditions, improved productivity, personal and collective recognition, constructive dialogue between staff and management… Everyone's a winner!

She has developed a simple initiative tailored to the circumstances of each of the various departments. The initiative has the approval of the board, which congratulated her and pledged its support. Ever since, ably assisted by the internal communications department, she has been constantly on the hoof promoting the project. Intranet, posters, company newsletter, management presentations, company-wide presentations… She has used every possible means of reaching every single employee.

Yet she has little to show for a year's hard work. It is true that a handful of departments have proposed a raft of innovations – innovations that have often yielded spectacular results. Yet elsewhere they have never even heard of 'Innovate for Change'. Kate is downcast: what on earth are they waiting for?

We have all found ourselves in Kate's situation at one time or another. We have made the effort to explain and to encourage an active response, only to discover that what we have said has not been heard. So how can intelligent people – like our people – claim not to know about plans and decisions when they have already been informed about them, sometimes repeatedly?

If your people did not hear you, maybe it is because they were not paying full attention, maybe it is because there is too much noise or maybe they are not operating on the same wavelength as you. Once you have identified the cause, you will be able to take action so as to ensure that they hear you better.

Talk their language and pique their curiosity

If your people have not heard you, maybe it is because you do not seem to be talking about what concerns them.

Mike is a sales rep at the public corporation where Kate works. When he sits down at his desk this morning, his objectives are: to clinch orders to meet his target (he is waiting to hear back on five quotes); to placate his customer after a major problem yesterday; and to expand his customer base (he has three visits to plan). There are also reports and other office procedures to take care of. He already has plenty on his plate. No, he is not familiar with the 'Innovate for Change' initiative. No, thanks, he does not really need to hear any more just now, as he is busy. Some other time, perhaps?

Kate interprets such a response as a lack of interest in or commitment to the company. Meanwhile, Mike feels that senior management and the head office people live in an ivory tower; they have no interest in his work and are out of touch with life at the coalface. How should Kate approach Mike in order to make herself heard?

We all know that when a company addresses its customers, for example through a mailshot, it does not talk about itself. Neither does it talk about its in-house concerns, its difficulties or its internal organization. It knows that customers want it to talk about them. Customers want a company to talk about their situation, their expectations and their difficulties and then to offer them a solution requiring them to take a series of simple actions: select, order and pay.

Yet, when we try to capture the attention of our own people, we do not always apply these principles. We talk about our objectives, our projects and our action plans. It is true that certain individuals feel a strong sense of attachment to their company (particularly senior executives, but people at other levels too), so such an approach works for them. However, such words simply go over the heads of other people.

In fact, seven months ago, Mike did indeed receive a document distributed by Kate entitled 'Innovate for Change initiative: implementation schedule'. This document began with a summary of project objectives and proceeded to give details as to how they could be achieved. Mike has forgotten that it even existed. Yet he would certainly have opened a document entitled 'Sales reps, give us your ideas!' Such a document could have had chapter headings like 'Clinch more orders', 'Satisfy your main customers', 'Expand your customer base' and 'Save time on reports'.

As managers, it is our responsibility to approach people in such a way that they appreciate that our subject is of direct concern to them, so that their attention doesn't wander.

Yet it is not always enough to ensure that your message is heard. Perhaps there is too much noise.

Talk less – but differently

Within companies, people receive a glut of information. E-mails, letters, meetings, discussions in the corridor or around the coffee machine, internet, intranet... people pick up a very large number of signals and messages. So how are they to distinguish what really matters?

Let us put ourselves in their place for a moment. Just imagine that you are taking part in your company's annual convention. At a quarter to nine, you settle down in the 37th row of an enormous 2,000-seat auditorium. You greet your colleagues as they arrive. You are enthusiastic. You love occasions like this. At nine o'clock, the lights are dimmed and the CEO opens the meeting. He announces a packed agenda, as usual. 'No early lunch today,' you say to yourself. After those few seconds of discouragement, you concentrate for a few minutes, for just long enough to hear the introduction and the company results for the past year. The agenda was packed with items, and now the slides are packed with data. What a nightmare! You cannot see very clearly from your seat.

Neither can you understand all the acronyms. After half an hour you are no longer really following what is being said. You hear the CEO's voice, but your mind is wandering. You have now clearly switched off.

Just then, the colleague on your right discreetly asks you about a project that you are working on together. You discuss the matter in hushed tones for a few minutes – it is so rare to get the chance to talk to one another. Just as the 100th slide is displayed, you notice another colleague, who is quietly sneaking in to take a seat near the door. You send her a text message to tease her about being late. She sends an amusing reply and in turn you rack your brain for a witty retort. As the 120th slide is displayed, your mobile vibrates. Maybe it is a customer or something important? You leave the auditorium to answer, only to discover that it is a minor supplier. It could have waited, but now that you are outside you deal with it… and while you are there you take the opportunity to go to the toilet.

When you re-enter the auditorium, the CEO is on the 190th slide. What a shame! You will never know it, but you have missed the presentation of the priorities for the year to come. That was slide number 182.

Information overload kills information. Attentive listeners cannot take more than 10 minutes of talk without their concentration drifting significantly.[1] A less focused individual may switch off in less than a minute. That is why mass media celebrity interviews set such a frantic pace with their questions and answers. A letter more than half a page long will not be read in full. Neither will an e-mail consisting of more than a few lines. So, if you have bought this book, you are one of a tiny minority of people who can cope with a text longer than your average e-mail.

Thus, to make yourself heard, you often need to talk less. Being concise takes time. As Pascal wrote apologetically in his Sixteenth Provincial Letter in 1656, 'I have only written at length because I did not have the time to write a shorter letter.'

ARE YOU PROVIDING ENOUGH
INFORMATION?

YOU SEND ME SO MUCH THAT I
CLASSIFIED IT AS SPAM

You also need to express yourself differently: surprise them; intrigue them; amuse them; rouse their curiosity. When a project is being implemented company-wide, there are numerous ways of achieving this: e-mails, posters, videos, in-house magazines, newsletters, intranet, T-shirts, pens, stickers, gadgets, etc. Yet, even within the smallest of units, nothing prevents the manager from taking a different approach to communicate with the team. For example, during a meeting, an administrative services manager might get people to stage a mock court hearing (dressed in wigs and gowns!) so as to 'indict' outdated procedures that need to be changed. A year later not a single participant will have forgotten the message transmitted on that occasion.

So you are talking less but differently, yet still some of your people have not heard you. No doubt that is because they are not operating on the same wavelength as you.

Tune in and turn on

Have you never asked yourself why some people seem to hang on your every word, while others seem to be completely indifferent? What if those people are quite simply operating on a different wavelength from you?

Let's face it, we are all different. What may be stimulating, convincing and motivating to one may be greeted by blank indifference from another. In particular, research carried out by specialists in neurolinguistic programming has demonstrated that there are several different types of perception, depending upon the individual, meaning that it is important to adapt to this if you want your voice to be heard. Let us look at a few of these modes of perception.

Firstly, some people are more focused on anticipated benefits (the 'target-driven' profile), whereas others are motivated more by avoiding problems (the 'risk avoidance' profile). This is a crucial distinction: practical experience has demonstrated that messages focusing on risks barely register with 'target-driven' people. Likewise, highlighting the anticipated benefits of an initiative will not allow you to grab the attention of an individual who possesses a 'risk avoidance' profile.

Secondly, what some people need above all is to understand the goal sought by a new initiative. In fact, they like to consider for themselves the different options that might allow them to achieve the objective. Yet, if the purpose is unclear, they will not register the details of the message transmitted to them. In contrast, other people can only grasp an objective if you explain to them exactly and specifically the different stages that will allow them to achieve it.

Lastly, while some of us are spontaneously interested in people, others are inspired more by processes. The former hear only discourse about humans, their thoughts and their emotions, while the latter register only points relating to tasks, systems and tools.

In any case, different verbal or written project presentations must include those items liable to be heard by all your people, whatever their profile. You must therefore demonstrate the anticipated advantages and the risks of inaction, clearly express the objective and the stages in achieving it, and refer both to processes and to people.

In short, as we saw in Chapter 1, even if your message is delivered it must also be received and understood. For that to happen, you need to talk to your people about themselves. You need to talk less but differently and must adapt your message to different modes of perception.

But is the fact that your message has been delivered and heard enough to ensure that it has also been received and understood? We shall address this theme in Chapter 3.

In conclusion to this chapter...

You have got the message: after having the courage to open the box of secrets, the second thing to do is to capture everyone's attention.

Take this book and give it to a friend. Ask your friend to put the following questions to you about the way in which you address those people you need in order to implement your project:

- Do you talk your people's language?

- Is your message addressed specifically to them?

    - Do you start by talking to them about themselves?

    - Do you make connections between your project and their own main concerns?

- Do you show them the extent to which they personally have a crucial role to play?

• Do you keep it brief, with a message that is short, clear and incisive?

• Do you address them in an original manner, adopting a distinctive, innovative tone?

• Do you operate on different wavelengths, with a message that is adapted to the different profiles of your people?

  - Do you talk to them both about the anticipated benefits and about the risks of inaction?

  - Have you clearly highlighted the goal that is to be achieved? Have you also specified the stages by which this will be achieved?

  - Does your message refer both to people and to tools, procedures and tasks?

If your friend seems unconvinced by your answers, you undoubtedly still have some work to do. Otherwise, well done! You can move on to the next chapter.

Note

1. Read *Brain Rules* by John Medina (Pear Press, Seattle, WA, 2009).

3 Spell it out in words of one syllable

Why don't people understand, even though it has been explained so clearly?

Think like a wise man but communicate in the language of the people.

William Butler Yeats, Irish poet, 1865–1939

Summary

You know the message and how to capture your people's attention. Let's look at how you can use the art of storytelling to lift your communication so that your people not only hear your messages but fully understand them. We'll show how to clearly construct your essential messages and how to build upon what is already happening in your business as a source of inspiration and the practical application of your strategy.

'What can you do? People here are only interested in technology.' At this subsidiary of a major energy group, senior management have never really communicated much with their staff, except about engineering and techie stuff. 'That's what they're interested in.'

Claudia, the COO, thinks that the time for that has passed. She reckons that they must now provide meaning. They must explain to middle managers and their people just what they are working towards – regardless of whether they are engineers, sales reps, accountants or machine operators. So one morning she takes the initiative and sets up a project group. Its mission is clear: to find the best means of explaining the company's objectives to all staff. The team gets down to work and designs an impressive communications tool.

Objectives are classified under four strategic issues: quality, growth, profitability and skills development. A single document offers an elegant presentation of these four issues (each one colour-coded) and breaks them down into 37 key indicators. It is all covered by a pretty chart with a simple slogan: 'Onwards to the Future!' Once it has the approval of the board, hundreds of posters are printed off and quickly displayed on every site, in every corridor and in most workshops and offices.

A few months later, the group carries out its annual employee opinion survey. Claudia is astonished to discover that more than 60 per cent of the staff (including 40 per cent of middle managers) claim to lack awareness of their corporate objectives.

With her colleague Neil, human resources director, she decides to carry out a further study, designed to see how the strategic objectives of 'Onwards to the Future!' relate to the individual goals assigned to each person at annual performance reviews. Once again, her jaw drops: there is almost no perceptible connection between the general objectives displayed on every noticeboard and the more specific goals recorded on annual review documents.

In the grand setting of the boardroom, beneath the gaze of the founder's bust, the board members are dismayed. The CEO is particularly furious: 'It's like having a football team and half of the players don't know where the goal is. It's incredible – and unacceptable.'

Gerry, the IT manager, goes further: 'We've stuck the objectives right in front of their faces – in their corridors, in their offices, in colour, with a slogan. What more do they want?' Another board member timidly intervenes: 'I think that I did tell you at the time: the people here are only interested in techie stuff.' 'That is not true,' Claudia retorts. 'They are desperate for meaning. Our people want to know. They want to understand. As far as I am concerned, the problem is that middle management have not yet bought into this strategy.'

The CEO expresses his irritation: 'But why do they not absorb anything we tell them… when Claudia has explained things so clearly?' Then, after a brief silence: 'What on earth are they waiting for?'

We all sometimes share the CEO's (fortunately brief) feelings of frustration and discouragement, when our people complain that nothing is ever explained and then never seem satisfied with any explanation that is provided.

As we saw in the first two chapters, a message must not only be delivered, but also be heard. Yet the fact that a message is heard does not necessarily mean that it has been understood. Staff surveys provide ample evidence of this. Despite the communications campaigns that are generally deployed, few employees believe that they have been properly informed about their organization's main aims. Still fewer say that they know how they personally can contribute to the aims.

So how can intelligent people fail to understand messages delivered to them by their senior managers? To answer this, we first need to identify at precisely what level the incomprehension exists. It may be located at two levels: either people simply do not understand the essence of the message that you are sending them or they do not appreciate that you are asking them to act.

Don't just give information: tell a story

If your people do not understand what they are told, maybe that is simply because the words used are inappropriate.

> 'You're suffering from a headache. I am prescribing acetylsalicylic acid.'

> 'Eh? Couldn't I just take an aspirin, doctor?'

How many of us have been blinded by science like this? How many of us have practically torn our hair out reading a computer manual:

> 'If you have a fixed IP address, use a WEP key to code your router.'

> 'What?'

Just because a message is clear to the person sending it (a doctor, a computer technician or a manager) does not mean that it is comprehensible to the recipient (the patient, a computer user or a junior employee). At a company, communications problems often stem simply from the language used.

Take a stroll along the corridors of the senior management floor and listen to the conversations. You will hear a multitude of words such as 'programme', 'market', 'project', 'vision', 'ambition', 'values', 'segments', 'approach', 'skills' and 'process'. In theory, these are simple words that anyone can easily understand, on this floor at least. Yet they are abstract. The people who use them almost all come from the same business management courses, for which they were selected precisely because of their ability to reason in an abstract manner. Over the years, those people have further reinforced this ability by handling concepts – and not physical objects – on a daily basis.

Now take the lift down to where front-line staff work. Prick up your ears again. The words that you hear will be much more specific: the new customer who has called; the product that must be delivered; the computer that has broken down; the colleague who needs assistance... This is the 'real' world, where company business is put into practice. Here, practical intelligence is the main quality required to resolve problems and satisfy customers. So, when managers talk about skills and processes, it is to be expected that their people will not immediately associate this with any very specific content. Furthermore, when presentations or e-mails are drafted in 'management-speak' ('line of business', 'horizontal management structures', 'alignment', 'matrices', etc), they are bound to switch off.

So, if you want to be understood, you must choose your words very carefully. But even this is not enough. You must also construct messages and tell stories.

Imagine a world without PowerPoint, computers, BlackBerries, mobile phones or landlines, a world in which all company managers are obliged to keep their hands tied behind their backs during working hours. It is an absurd idea, of course. Yet, in all probability, it would be a world in which communications would quickly become more effective. Indeed, if every morning we had to explain to our people in just a few words (shouting to get heard above the din) just what we wanted to achieve, we would get straight to the point. 'Straight to the point' equates to our message, which we want our people to understand and remember.

A message will be 3 to 10 words, including a specific verb and a clear meaning.

A slide presenting a statistical table under the title 'First quarter sales trends' does not convey any message. Each person viewing that slide will interpret it differently. 'That doesn't look good,' thinks one person. 'Things aren't as bad as I feared,' says another. 'That's strange, that brief sales surge in April,' comments a third.

In contrast, a slide announcing 'Our sales fell even faster in the first quarter,' illustrated by a simple graph, leaves no room for doubt. Whether at a meeting, one to one or in writing, communications with our people should be stripped down to an essential message. The message is the essence of what you have to say, expressed as simply and clearly as possible.

A message can be broken down into three or four secondary messages, each with the same characteristics: 3 to 10 words, including a specific verb and a clear meaning. These messages can be supported by illustrations, explanations or figures, or they in turn can be broken down into sub-messages, subject to the same conditions. However, the essential message must be presented from the outset, and it must be regularly repeated and reaffirmed.

Let us be honest. Sometimes we are incapable of spontaneously reducing our words to three or four elementary messages: 'Reality is more complex'; 'Things are more subtle'; 'We must adopt a more nuanced approach'; etc. If that is the case, in truth it is because we have not done our work yet: we have not made the effort to decide what we want to express. We have not identified what our people really must understand and remember. We are passing the buck and getting them to do the work that we have failed to carry out.

So we need to identify and to formulate clear, logical messages. This is crucial, but more is required, because experience shows that humans are not ideally set up to understand logic; they are ideally set up to understand stories.[1]

When Muhammad Yunus, the Nobel Peace Prize winner, explains how he invented microcredit, he starts by telling the story of Sufia, a mother from a shanty town in Bangladesh who made stools. In order to rescue her family from long-term poverty, Sufia needed a loan that she could not obtain. Yunus recounts his moving dialogue with this woman and her husband, before telling how he met another 26 families who found themselves in a similar situation. He then tells of his meeting with a local banker. This financier reckoned that it would be absurd to lend to people who were offering no repayment guarantee and that in any case you cannot turn a profit from very small loans. Yunus expresses his helplessness. The total value of the loans required to save these 27 families from poverty was less than 15 dollars. When Muhammad Yunus goes on to convey his essential messages on the role of microcredit, he has the rapt attention of his audience. When he finishes his speech, his audience usually give him a standing ovation.

In order to encourage a team to work tirelessly to achieve customer satisfaction, you can present statistics, indicators and principles. Alternatively, you can start by giving a lively account of a recent conversation with a customer. Describe what happened, provoke laughter at the ridiculous nature of the situation, express your embarrassment at errors made and encourage feelings of pride when the customer expresses gratitude for the work done by the team. Then get your message across.

In short, if your people do not understand what they are told, check that you are using simple and specific words, that your message is crystal clear and can be expressed in a few words, and that it is illustrated by a lively and meaningful story. People will understand.

They then need to understand that they have a role to play in all this.

Spell it out: show them they must act

In the wake of the staff survey showing that 60 per cent of her people claimed not to understand their employer's objectives, Claudia collects a few personal accounts. How can a middle manager claim not to be aware of those objectives, when they are displayed on the corridor that he walks down at least 10 times a day? A departmental supervisor explains: 'Oh, yes, the posters! But those are senior management posters, you know. They are intended for customers who visit our premises. On the front line, we have our own problems to deal with and our own priorities to concentrate on.'

To ensure that your people understand that they are being asked to act, you need to adapt your message to their level, to present specific examples of things that they can do and to tell them how they can follow through on this.

Winning new customers is a tricky task for a small IT service company offering the personal touch, so building up customer loyalty and developing business from existing customers are a top priority. Alan, the newly appointed boss, is launching a project designed to increase the company's customer loyalty rating (number of customers retained from one year to the next) from 70 per cent to 80 per cent over two years. Three months after the launch of his project, Alan finds that little has changed, although everyone sees the need to win customer loyalty. Many of his people scrutinize the indicators every month in the hope of seeing a rise in the customer loyalty rating. Yet, when it comes down to specifics, no one has really done very much to contribute to the achievement of this objective. Alan is troubled by this.

The following Monday, at the management committee meeting, he asks his team for their views. The strategic project of winning customer loyalty is broken down into a simple action plan for each job (eg account manager, technical consultant or support staff). Thus, by the end of the month, all account managers must contact each of their five main customers and offer to organize a project review meeting. All of the management committee members are soon explaining the action plan to their teams, presenting a schedule and giving a personal commitment to its implementation. As each person now has a series of specific, achievable and meaningful tasks, they quickly swing into action. The response is so rapid that just a few weeks later Alan is wondering whether a customer loyalty target of 80 per cent is not 'setting our sights a bit low' after all.

In practice, you are deluding yourself if you believe that everyone will grasp a very general message and spontaneously convert it into specific initiatives. To be understood, you must convey your message in different ways so as to ensure that it is specifically applicable to each staff category. Likewise, the schedule can be broken down into shorter periods, allowing each individual to think up more tangible and immediate initiatives.

Yet this is still not enough to ensure that people understand that they must act: you must also offer your people practical examples.

At a service company, on the same day, two regional offices launch the group's quality project.

Patrick, the first regional manager, presents the objectives and the project. He has then arranged for an expert to talk about successive approaches to quality management in various industries over the past 20 years. A welter of statistics allows him to compare the approaches preferred by business sector and by country. The regional quality manager then details the various processes under consideration, highlighting the indicators now in use. For his part, the regional manager explains the respective roles of quality managers, auditors, team managers and other staff. They then work in subgroups to help everyone to memorize the main procedures with which they need to be familiar.

At the other regional office, Louise, the manager, takes a different approach. To illustrate each of the three project priorities, she calls on a staff member or supervisor to present an initiative that has already been introduced. Thus, Nick explains how he wanted to handle customer claims better, how he refined the rules on handling applications and how he was able to accurately measure the progress made. Naturally, it was at this second regional office that the project bedded in more quickly: all staff members understood that they were being asked to act.

Lastly, of course, for your people to understand that they need to take action, it is important to talk to them about what comes next: what are the short-term objectives and how can they be followed up? These issues will be examined in detail in Chapters 10 and 11.

Now let us return to Claudia and her 'Onwards to the Future!' project. The next managers' convention is scheduled to take place in a few weeks' time, and Claudia's resolve is firm: they need to change the format of that half-day event. Previously, at these conventions, the 200 delegates would listen to a long speech by the CEO, who would mainly review the corporation's various technical projects. As a gifted orator, the CEO knew how to make these subjects exciting. He could captivate his audience, which had never complained about the format traditionally used for the event.

This time, however, Claudia wants to change things around. Her idea is a simple one: after a brief introduction by the CEO, to start by tackling head on the issue of the suitability of the strategy and to humbly acknowledge that the objectives have not been understood. To achieve this, she has no hesitation in resorting to humour. She simply arranges for the filming of a few short video clips in which managers are seen implementing the strategy, each in their distinctive style: selecting objectives by drawing lots, eccentric interpretations of slogans, etc. Claudia achieves her objective: the audience is amused, and its curiosity is aroused.

She then moves on to a short section explaining how the strategy had been constructed. She presents her diagnosis of the situation, relying upon the results of in-house interviews carried out by consultants. What is missing and what do we need to do? She thereby shows managers that their views have been heard and that they will receive assistance. She also encourages them to take the reins in their own sections so as to take ownership of the strategy and to promote it.

No doubt the third part of the convention is the key moment. Claudia has arranged for contributions from several managers and workers who have regularly set a good example in implementing and promoting the strategy. So the audience hears a section supervisor give a simple explanation as to how he motivated his team by tailoring each of the corporation's strategic objectives to individual monthly work plans. Then an engineer and an IT specialist describe their collaboration on a project to introduce an information system, thereby illustrating their contribution to performance objectives. Lastly, a PA stands on the stage to tell how, since her manager showed her the connections between her work and the corporation's strategic objectives, she had been strongly motivated by the meaning that she saw in her everyday duties.

The audience bursts into spontaneous applause. Claudia has pulled it off. She follows this up by presenting the contribution expected from managers: to get the strategy out there and to ensure that their people understand it. In order to achieve this, she provides them with a motivational package for use at team meetings. The initiative has been properly launched and the final element, a competition to find a name for the plan, stimulates great interest. Two months later, most team meetings have taken place. The information has got around. The posters are even more prominent, because the people themselves have put them up near their workstations. 'Onwards to the Future!' has become a permanent feature of daily life for teams.

In short, to ensure that your message is understood, it also needs to be clear, and all members of staff need to know very specifically what action they must take and how they must take it.

Let us suppose that your message has been delivered, heard and understood. Is that enough to ensure that it is accepted? We shall look at that in Chapter 4.

In conclusion to this chapter…

You have got it: after daring to open the box of secrets and capturing everyone's attention, your third key task is to spell the message out to them in words of one syllable: to express yourself in such a way that you are fully understood.

Take this book and give it to one of your colleagues. Ask your colleague to put the following questions to you:

- Your message has been delivered and heard, but are you sure that it has also been properly understood?

- Are the words you use clear and specific?

- Have you thought up three or four essential messages, each comprising:

  - no more than 3 to 10 words;

  - a specific verb; and

  - a complete lack of ambiguity?

- Do you take the trouble to tell people a story, rather than just to inform them, when you talk to them about your project? If so:

- Is the story moving?

- Is it funny?

- Does it allow each individual to fully understand and remember what you hope to achieve together?

● Have you 'spelt it out to them'? Have people really understood that they are being asked to take action?

- Has your general message been specially tailored to each category of people or even to each individual concerned?

- Have your people been shown specific examples of initiatives taken by particular colleagues?

- Have you assigned short-term objectives to each individual and presented how these can be followed up?

If your colleague seems confused by your answers, you still have some work to do. Otherwise, move on to the next chapter.

Note

1. This expression was used by Roger Schank, a cognitive sciences specialist from the University of Chicago.

4 Mould opinion

Here's why they don't all agree with you, even though you're right

Leadership is the art of getting someone else to do something you want done because he wants to do it.

Dwight D Eisenhower

Summary

So your people have heard and understood what you want but are still not implementing your strategy. We'll explain why understanding and accepting a message are two entirely different behaviours and the most common reasons for non-acceptance. We demonstrate why words alone are not enough and the options you have at your disposal to mould your people's opinions so they act because they really want to.

'We really have very little time to get organized. If we do the same as we did two years ago, we're heading for disaster.' Jack is stressed out. His colleagues on the sales team lower their heads. They all know that something must be done – but what, and how? 'Two years ago, we failed to push through a price increase, and the results were disastrous.' Jack is determined not to make the same mistake again.

As the sales and marketing manager of a large corporation in the B2B sector, Jack has been here before. Margins have been crumbling under pressure from their customers' purchasing departments. More than half the company's turnover comes from large account contracts at low prices. The gross profit from some customers has slumped to 5 per cent, and that's before taking into account staff and training costs, admin, and operational and HQ overheads. The wage bill has to be paid each month, but customers are often taking 60 days to pay.

Even worse has been the turmoil at the top. With the share price falling, the major shareholder has kicked out the young CEO. The new boss has come in with a simple and logical idea: increase prices by 10 per cent with immediate effect. A letter needs to go out to all customers within six weeks, advising them of the new prices. Jack now has to get his sales team onside.

Jack, however, has got a problem. Two years ago, the same policy was tried. It didn't work. Customers were lost, contracts were cancelled and competitors enjoyed a windfall. Management backed down and then reversed the price hike. Utter humiliation. So what's different now?

The economic downturn has hit every business. Jack's sales reps are facing a new kind of argument from buyers: 'You are a big business; you have enormous financial muscle and yet all you ever try to do is to boost your profits off the back of customers like us.' His reps are telling him: 'This is not the time to be increasing prices.' The regional managers are blunter still: 'No way!'; 'Crazy idea!'; 'It'll never work!' Some go further: 'Once upon a time, there was respect for customers, and service meant something. These days, the only thing that senior management wants from us is ever more profit; nothing else matters.'

At the sales meeting, Jack is persuasive. 'Margins are crumbling; profits are down,' he tells them. 'If the price rise doesn't go ahead, the company will collapse, and we'll all lose our jobs.'

It's a compelling argument, but the sales team are shaking their heads. At the end of the meeting, he takes Natalie, his marketing manager, to one side. She tells him, 'They hear what you are saying, they understand the consequences of not putting through the price increase, but you haven't convinced them.'

Jack asks, 'When is the letter due to go out?'

'Six weeks,' she replies, 'but nothing's been done yet.'

Jack shakes his head in dismay. 'What on earth are they waiting for?'

We can understand why Jack might feel temporarily discouraged. He's made his case forcefully, his logic is impeccable, they've understood what he is saying, and yet he hasn't succeeded in getting his message across. Why not?

On a poster, a human-shaped robot taps away at a computer. The slogan above reads: 'Here is an employee with no ethnic origin, no sexual orientation and no political opinions who will never ask for a pay rise.'[1] The company that designed this campaign knew all too well that life would be much easier for top managers if staff didn't exist, because people are not content to just roll up their sleeves and do the work expected of them; they also have minds of their own.

For example, 1,500 company managers worldwide were asked about the main obstacles to change.[2] Only 8 per cent of them cited technological limitations, whereas 58 per cent referred to the difficulty of changing mindsets and behaviour. What is it with staff? First, they don't (won't?) listen to what they're told. Then, when they do listen, they don't understand a thing. Even worse, though, when they do understand they don't always agree, even though you're obviously right. So now we know the real reason for management setbacks: resistance to change.

We are going to start by looking at the reasons why your people may complain about decisions. We then go on to examine five principles that will allow you to overcome this major obstacle.

So what are they unhappy about? The exasperating aspect of resistance to change is that you cannot put it all down to ignorance or stupidity. In fact, within an organization, who puts up the most resistance? It is very often the people who are the most highly qualified, the most experienced and the best informed.

So why would intelligent people reject change? It is generally for one of these three reasons: they don't really believe in the problem that you want to resolve; they are not convinced that you have come up with the right solution; or the change in the pipeline conflicts with some of their interests or some of their values.

They don't believe that the problem exists

If they don't really believe that the problem exists, this is quite simply because they have a different perception from yours.

The celebrated Canadian management guru Professor Henry Mintzberg compares a company to a geometric circle: around the circumference are those members of staff who are in direct contact with customers and suppliers. Each of them has a very specific, detailed view of their role, but from a very limited viewpoint. In the middle of the circle, top managers have a much wider view of the organization's business, but without having an in-depth understanding of certain practical aspects of it.

Thus some problems are obvious to front-line staff, yet invisible to management. A young customer relations representative in a call centre receives three serious complaints from customers in a single day. They are furious at how difficult it is to install their new package. But what do management back at head office see? They see a slight drop in customer satisfaction indicators – and one that affects only a single product within the range.

The opposite is also true. Managers may notice that profitability is falling behind that of competitors. They may anticipate the arrival of new technology in the market or foresee that the market is going to focus on new customer segments. Even the best member of front-line staff, fully devoted to the resolution of problems that the manager does not fully understand, may be unaware of any such phenomena.

A single problem may also be interpreted in different ways. 'Our product is too expensive, so we are losing customers,' complains a sales rep. 'Our sales force is costing us too much, so our price is no longer competitive,' comments the finance director. Same starting point; different interpretation.

Lastly, just because you recognize that a problem exists does not mean that you necessarily devote your attention to resolving it. Let's take an example: a particular building does not comply with the official guidelines. The perimeter wall is not high enough. There are probably a lot of people on the ground who know that, to comply with those guidelines, the wall should be five metres high and not four, as it is currently. But there has never been any problem: on a practical level, the wall certainly seems to be quite high enough – and, in any case, the company does not have the budget required to implement every single guideline to the letter. A few months later, the boss of San Francisco Zoo states: 'We do not understand how the tiger could have escaped and killed a visitor: in theory, it was impossible.'[3]

It is not enough for people to recognize that a problem exists. They must also see what is at stake. What will happen if nothing is done? What are the real consequences and what are the risks? On the other hand, what opportunities might there be to tackle the problem? It has been established that in 60 per cent of crashes involving airliners in the United States, the instrument panel was clearly showing that there was a problem. On each occasion, the crew neglected to report this, as they did not believe that an accident could happen.

At Jack's company, how could staff spontaneously grasp the scale of the problem of shrinking margins and comprehend the challenges, opportunities and risks? For them, it wasn't all bad: it was true that gross margins had shrunk, but the business was continuing to rack up healthy profits worldwide. The share price had fallen, but only after four years continuously on the up. It was true that there had been a change of CEO, but that happened everywhere.

To summarize: if your message is not really accepted, perhaps it is because your people do not believe that the problem you are trying to resolve really exists.

They don't believe in the solution

If your people are not convinced that you have come up with the right solution, they have no reason to rally around in order to put it into practice.

First scenario: the problem is seen as insoluble, so why wear yourself out implementing solutions that are doomed to fail? The result is that only the most obedient employees apply your instructions to the letter, and they do so without enthusiasm, idealism, energy or creativity. Worse than useless! A variation on this: yes, the problem can be solved – but the solution is not here. It is there – at head office or in another department – or it is the responsibility of a customer, a supplier, a partner or someone else. Why are you asking us to sort the problems out when the solutions lie elsewhere?

Here is another situation: yes, in the eyes of staff, the solution put forward by management allows the problem to be resolved, but another more effective or less painful solution has been overlooked. This is collective delusion syndrome: 'But all we have to do is to [choose one of the following as appropriate: cut prices, raise prices, employ more staff, take over our competitors, etc].' There is a variation on this theme, too: yes, solutions exist, but everyone has their own idea – a bit like selecting the national football team.[4]

At Jack's company, many members of staff probably understand the need to beef up margins. However, some of them believe that they should concentrate on major accounts and leave small customers alone – or the opposite. Others see it as a terrible mistake to send out a letter without warning: they should negotiate on a case-by-case basis, over a period of several months. Then again, others are convinced that only a revised range of services could allow pricing policy to be adjusted for particular customer segments. Others again are persuaded that falling prices are a problem that should be converted into an opportunity and that they should cut prices further in order to put certain competitors out of business so as to bring some order back into the marketplace.

Final potential scenario: yes, the solution presented is probably effective, but the price to be paid seems too high. The human cost seems unfair. Surely there must be other solutions. What are they? Well, it's up to top management to find out.

In short, if your message does not win people over, it might just be because your people do not believe that the solution that you want to implement is the right one.

The decision taken conflicts with some of their interests or values

Within Jack's organization, sales reps' pay includes a large variable element, based specifically on turnover. By informing customers of a sharp price rise, sales reps are therefore running the risk of losing orders and seeing their pay cut at the end of the month. In contrast, they have almost nothing to gain: as their profit targets have been revised sharply upwards, they will merely receive the same bonus if the company does increase its profitability. So the decision announced by management is clearly contrary to their interests. If their anticipated earnings fall, how are they going to afford the new car and the exotic holiday?

So Jack's staff have no desire to go and inform their customers of a price rise, because to do so goes against what they believe in: 'Once upon a time, people showed respect to customers and service meant something. These days, the only thing that senior management wants from us is ever more profits.'

Today more than ever, the individual is on a quest for meaning.[5] So your staff will ponder the following questions: Are our plans fundamentally right? Is it worth the hassle? Can we proudly tell our nearest and dearest about it?

Of course, anything can be put down to 'values'. Almost every social group will embrace a noble cause to further its own interests. Nevertheless we have to accept that, unlike a computer or a hydraulic press, employees have to deal with values that often conflict with one another. On the one hand, they quite often have a desire to serve the company and be loyal to a line manager, and a need to look after their families and keep their jobs. On the other hand, there is almost always a feeling of solidarity with people or other staff upset by change, an attachment to products, services and a particular way of doing the job, pride in work done in the past, etc.

It is not easy for a senior manager to recognize the 'noble' motives of those opposing plans that are sometimes crucial to a company's development or even to its survival. Resistance to change is generally put down to a blinkered view of a situation and a desire to defend personal interests against the general interest. This is true, yet the opposite can also be the case: a desire to defend values perceived as timeless against measures seen as motivated solely for short-term considerations.

In short, if your message wins little acceptance, maybe it is because your staff are driven to defend their interests – or are grappling with a conflict of values.

Ask yourself these questions. In a few simple words, what are the interests and values that might be – or might appear to be – threatened by the plan that you intend to implement? Which groups of staff are most likely to be sensitive to such threats?

I hear you say, 'Hang on a minute. I've already worked incredibly hard on this: firstly, to ensure that our message is understood throughout our organization and within every team, every institution and every country; secondly, to ensure that the message is understood by people of all ages, occupations and cultures. Now you're telling me that this message must also be accepted? Would it not be better to just bulldoze it through?'

Bulldozing a project through is not a good idea. If you need confirmation, try being a fly on the wall and spend some time with one of your teams, perhaps during the lunch break. You will soon encounter three of the main enemies of your project.

Your first adversary is despondency, expressed in hunched shoulders and sighs, in gloomy discussions and lifeless expressions. Of course, you need fear no violent outbursts. Everyone does their job. But the job is done slowly and without enthusiasm. No great creativity is applied to problem solving, and no one dreams of success. Such a lack of optimism is as harmful to a business as it is to a hospital patient or a sportsperson. Indeed, to expect failure is to invite it. We'll look at optimism again in Chapter 12.

Your second enemy is irony. This takes the form of sarcastic jokes, sniggering and muttered asides. Just what you need! You certainly created a true rapport among your people. The only problem is that it is directed against you. While humour can be a great tonic for team spirit, it can also presage serious problems when it is expressed at the expense of your business and its projects.

Your third opponent is anger. With clenched teeth and expressionless faces, in harsh voices and acrimonious words, your people are letting you know what they think in no uncertain terms. All very well perhaps, but anger is contagious and can even turn into blind rage. This can be expressed to differing degrees, through open hostility, hard-line militancy, the posting of virulent criticism on external websites, and even deliberate sabotage of company initiatives.

Your worst enemy, however, is probably indifference. You encounter no open opposition, no stormy debates, no sarcastic comments and no signs of despondency. On the contrary, life goes on as before. In other words, nothing ever changes.

So you cannot bulldoze a project through. You need the committed support of a sufficient proportion of your people to gradually bring all the others on board. You need to win acceptance for your message, but how? Obviously, there is no miraculous way of generating widespread support for a project, particularly if it requires change and hard work. However, five simple principles may be of assistance to you.

Come on! Put yourself in their shoes for a minute

When placed within an organization, individuals tend to adopt extraordinarily rational patterns of behaviour. Thus, the first thing to do, in order to win the support of a group of people for a plan of action, is to understand how these people see things from their perspective. In other words, how would we see things if we put ourselves in their shoes? Given our personal history, our environment, what we know and what we do not, does the problem really seem important? Does the intended solution seem appropriate? Are our interests threatened? Are values that are important to us being undermined?

Naturally, the people concerned do not constitute a homogeneous mass. You need to analyse these questions by establishing appropriate segmentation, whether by positions held within the organization, by sociological factors (age, seniority, etc) or by more behavioural criteria, such as the disparity often evident between 'old-fashioned' and 'forward-looking' staff.

One of the first results of such thinking is that it allows you to identify your potential allies and opponents, not forgetting the intermediate group who adopt a 'wait-and-see' approach and who are liable to switch from one side to the other, depending upon the turn of events. All specialists in change quite correctly explain that you need to avoid focusing on your opponents and that it is essential to mobilize your allies in order to win over the waverers.

However, if the success of your initiative requires everyone to truly take ownership of it, you need to go much further either in your in-house briefings or in the way that the project itself is designed, with four potential objectives. For some people you can either reduce the advantages of the current situation or increase the benefits that they will glean from your plan. You can also either increase the disadvantages in the status quo or reduce the constraints associated with the implementation of your action plan. If you really put yourself in your people's shoes, you will immediately sense that it is the 'positive' options designed to provide advantages rather than constraints that offer much more motivation.

Yet it is not enough to put yourself in others' shoes, because others are observing us as we carry out our true role: so what sort of an example are we setting?

Stop moaning and set an example

At the end of 2008, for the first time ever, the major US car makers found themselves on the verge of bankruptcy, crippled by the credit crisis and the collapse of the automotive market. They announced drastic cutbacks: reductions in production capacity, slashing support functions, mass redundancies, elimination of company benefits, etc. In order to obtain the support of their staff and management, their message relied upon indisputable facts and figures. This also came accompanied with the promise of a better future, with the development of innovative, eco-friendly products to suit new market expectations.

However, one detail radically altered the perception of many employees: when they went to Washington to persuade the federal authorities to assist the automotive sector, the three bosses of GM, Ford and Chrysler arrived… in their private jets. This means of transport is commonplace in the United States, especially for the senior managers of mega-corporations. In fact, it is the most flexible (and often the most economical) means of transport for criss-crossing the globe throughout the year. However, in this context, it made the key words 'cost cuts' unacceptable to many employees – and pretty lacking in credibility among politicians. The following month, for another visit to the Senate, the three top executives travelled the 500 miles from Detroit to Washington in tiny prototype electric cars. It was a commendable effort, if somewhat belated.

In contrast, when Jean-Marie Descarpentries took charge at Bull, a leading Paris-based IT company wrestling with colossal losses, he adopted simple personal measures to set an example. He refused to move into the senior management floor, the top storey of the Tour Bull skyscraper at La Défense. He asked for a small office in the middle of the office tower and found himself in the middle of a sales department. As for his company car, he asked to swap his Renault Safrane for a Laguna, a more economical model, and announced that he would have no need for a chauffeur, unlike his predecessors. Those symbolic measures had a considerable impact. His planned cutbacks, which unlike the five previous plans did not include any compulsory redundancies without compensation, were widely deployed throughout the corporation, producing spectacular results.

In general, what you say is less important than what you do. If you do not practise the values that you preach, you will have little influence.

Sorting things out from the top down: get your middle managers onside first

Karina, a customer relations representative at a call centre, was initially convinced by an internal briefing from senior management: improve customer service; respond more fully to each customer's needs; and provide proactive, customized follow-up. It all sounded good. The slogans and photos available over the intranet also presented a great image of call centres.

Then this morning, when she asked Steve, her departmental manager, just when this initiative was to be launched on their site, he didn't even need to open his mouth to discourage her. All he needed to do was to give a knowing laugh and a weary wave of his hand. She understood right away: 'Oh... You don't need to worry yourself about it: we'll do it, but it won't be of any use, other than to create further problems. The IT isn't ready; marketing don't know what they're doing. It's the same old story.'

Within your company, all you need is one Steve to discourage 10 Karinas. That is why it is essential that you should get all your middle managers on your side. Eighty per cent of your internal marketing work must be directed at that 20 per cent of your staff.

Clearly, within a large organization, management encompasses very different levels of responsibility and personal profiles. You must start at the top, ensuring that you have the support of your senior executives. Indeed, even if they do not always have the capacity to effectively deploy your strategy, you may rest assured that they are certainly in a position to torpedo any of your initiatives: generally, inaction on their part will suffice. Every tier of management must then be dealt with specifically in succession. In fact, it is crucial that each tier feels that it is being given some responsibility for its own staff.

Of course, within large corporations it is generally seen as good form to criticize middle managers: 'There are too many tiers of management.' 'Local management is not playing its part.' Some plans can also usefully be based upon parallel networks ('project ambassadors', 'task force leaders', etc). However, when rolling out a strategic initiative for the long term, it is crucial that you can count on management support. Part 3 of this book is entirely devoted to dealing with these issues.

As for how to achieve this, the principles are the same as for all other staff. Let's have a look at them.

Open the windows: let your message come from outside, too

Bosses delivering an uplifting message are often suspected of partiality. In the eyes of staff, they are assumed to be biased, and their message is treated as propaganda. They exaggerate the benefits of their plan and play down the disadvantages. Actually, such a scenario is comparatively rare, but it can happen.

In contrast, the direct and authentic testimony of an outsider is viewed differently.

A classic means of achieving this is to call on an expert. As consultants, we often have to play this role at corporate events. It is striking to see to what extent a statistic or mere anecdote can change minds, when this is reported by a person perceived (sometimes correctly) as experienced, competent and objective. Suddenly it is as if the manager's message had been sanctified, validated, made irrefutable.

How about a more impressive method? Use a customer, a genuine customer, a professional, someone who knows the business and its products – someone, too, who sees competitors and compares the services provided.

We have used this method recently at our company. Of all the species on the planet, consultants are definitely a breed apart – along with journalists and film stars. Whatever the subject or the situation, they possess a rare ability to dismiss the solutions offered as utterly unsuitable and totally inappropriate. To make matters worse, they will advise you that the problem has not been correctly stated in the first place.

So should you give consultants the impression that their recommendations need to be more suited to each customer's particular circumstances? That would be an insult. This is where your customer intervenes, in the flesh, in the shape of four senior executives from major corporations that are customers of your company.

Divided into eight teams, within two hours the consultants had to develop recommendations, based on specific customer concerns. The teams then have to compete with one another, in twos, each presenting their recommendation to one of the customers present.

Without further ado, the customer then poses questions, raises objections and arguments, and then announces a decision. The customers use specific real-life examples to explain to the whole room just why a 'customized' service is essential to them. The impact of this is enormous.

Whether experts or customers, your external witnesses must fulfil a few conditions in order to support your message. Firstly, it is preferable that they should not represent a group that is loathed by your staff – unless they are very powerful. Secondly, they should offer personal, credible experience. They must be capable of expressing themselves clearly and unambiguously. And, last but not least, they must be completely convinced that you have a valid message.

In what other way could information from outside convey your message? Cover some of your walls with images and statistics giving a view of the market. Place your competitors' new products in your display cases. Use your intranet to show or broadcast video reports illustrating the challenges that you wish people to address.

In short, by opening the windows, you allow in a breath of fresh air that will reinvigorate your message.

Hold your head up high and appeal to values

When Jack has to address 300 of his branch managers, he doesn't spare them the truth: the need to increase margins, the pressure of the financial markets and the desire of shareholders to obtain a better return on capital investment. Yet he also takes great care to give them other reasons to rally behind him: 'Look at the work that your teams do and the work that you do. Just think how together we have increased the quality of service that we have offered our customers over the past 10 years. Remember how you work harder and harder to meet difficult, urgent and complicated requests. Then ask yourself: is it right that the price of these services should fall year by year? Is it right that the customer should pay less and less, while you provide more and more?' In the hall, their faces light up. Why? Because the branch managers have just grasped that there is a meaning to their struggle for greater margins. Defending shareholders, an anonymous, amorphous mass of certificate holders enriching themselves in their sleep? Not exactly the most exciting rallying call. Supporting your own team, its professionalism and its hard work: that's something else. Yet it is the same struggle.

Companies have their own values. These are not always the same as the ones displayed on walls and in leaflets, which sometimes relate more to the aspirations of the CEO than the soul of the organization. They are deep-rooted beliefs that have been shared by staff for years, if not decades. Above all, within a particular business sector, particular corporate entities may share ideals of being the best. Some may value marketing innovation, growth and breaking into new markets. Others may worship outstanding technical performance. Yet others will feel that customer service is the noblest calling.

A single project may bring a range of values into play. Highlight those that form part of your company's culture and you will give meaning to your people's working lives. In other words, to win support for change, you also need to place a high value on things that don't change.

Many managers err by continually talking about change and stressing that nothing will be the same again. Firstly, they err in substance, because most core activities remain remarkably stable. In the car industry, despite recurrent debates about oil prices, global warming and traffic gridlock, what has really changed fundamentally over the past century? General car design (internal combustion engine, wheels, bodywork, key functions, etc) has not changed; neither has the commercial distribution system, nor even the main marketing claims. Since the latter part of the 19th century, particular retail formats have developed, methods and techniques have become more sophisticated (category management, efficient customer response (ECR), etc) and products have been sold online, but the keys to success still remain the same: ease of access, the choice and quality of products, the personalization of customer service and competitive pricing. Even in the world of high tech, where one revolution seems to follow another, fundamental trends remain remarkably consistent, to the extent that Jeff Bezos, founder and CEO of Amazon.com, is able to explain that, from the outset, he built his strategy exclusively upon 'things that won't change'.[6]

In particular, managers err about method, because staff can accept a change only if they understand what will not be changing. They are so much more accepting of a message foretelling a change if that message abides by their values.

In conclusion to this chapter...

So now you have understood: having dared to open the box of secrets, captured individuals' attention and painted them a picture, the fourth key element of the energy of engagement is to mould opinion, to eliminate the main objections to a decision.

Take this book and offer it to a 10-year-old. Ask the 10-year-old to put the following questions to you:

● What exactly is the problem that you want to solve?

● And do the people you work with think that it is a problem too?

● … and have they understood the cause of the problem?

● … and do they think that the problem is amazingly important too?

● In a nutshell, what is the solution that you want to offer them?

● And do the people you work with also think that it is a great solution to their amazingly important problem?

- Deep down, do the people you work with believe that what you want to get them to do is a good thing or a bad thing?

- Do they think that it is nasty to do something like that to them?

- When they go home, are they proud to talk about it or a bit ashamed?

- Have you put yourself in their shoes for a bit?

- Have you properly identified your allies, with whom you will win other allies over to your cause?

- Have you changed things so as to get more allies on your side?

- Do you sometimes stop complaining and set everyone an example yourself?

- Are you sure that you are walking the walk as well as talking the talk?

- Are you sorting things out from the top down? Are you dealing with the bosses first? Do the bosses you are in charge of really want to help you?

- Oh! Not all of them do? So what are you doing to make sure that they really, really want to?

- Are you 'opening windows'? Aren't there people outside your company – you know, in the normal world – who could help you to explain things to them?

- How about if you held your head up high and explained to them that it is a great idea and that they can be proud of it, wouldn't that help them to come around and agree with you?

- It would? So how are you going to achieve that?

If the 10-year-old doesn't immediately understand your answers, you still have some work to do.[7] Otherwise, great! You can move on to the next chapter.

Notes

1. Campaign created in 2008 by CLM BBDO for Adia.
2. Making Change Work study, IBM, 2008.
3. Reported by Agence France Presse on 26 December 2007 and 31 December 2007.
4. Read the box 'The boss is always wrong', in 'When teams can't decide', by Bob Frisk, *Harvard Business Review*, November 2008, on the near statistical impossibility of satisfying the majority of staff where several solutions are put forward.
5. Read, *inter alia, Man's Search for Meaning*, by Viktor Frankl (Washington Square Press, New York, 1984), which claims that an individual's primary motivation is neither pleasure nor power but meaning.
6. Read the excellent article 'The institutional yes: an interview with Jeff Bezos', by Julia Kirby and Thomas A Stewart, in *Harvard Business Review*, October 2007.
7. 'If you can't explain a concept to a 6-year-old, you don't fully understand it' (Albert Einstein).

5 Provide an emotional spark

Why are they dragging their feet when they know that they need to act?

Nothing great in the world has ever been accomplished without passion.

Hegel

Summary

Your people have started to act, but often projects get difficult and bogged down. The harder things become, the more managers tend to listen less and demand more. We'll look at innovative ways to maintain energy by ensuring your people feel understood and above all appreciated. We'll explore how to use emotion as a powerful tool in galvanizing your people towards a common purpose. Finally, we'll demonstrate how to drive strategy implementation from the front by managing the impact of your own behaviour and attitude.

Stefan is a business unit director for a large industrial conglomerate. Distributed across 27 countries, his teams manufacture and sell construction equipment and are market leaders. Many local competitors are entering this market and flooding it with cheap products. The most price-sensitive customers are attracted to these suppliers. This applies, in particular, to industrial firms intending to build new warehouses and to certain project managers tendering for major construction schemes. Other customers, more sensitive to quality and design, are remaining loyal to Stefan's teams and would probably even be prepared to accept higher prices if necessary. This certainly applies to architects working on residential housing projects.

Thus, in order to continue to deliver profitable growth, with his team, Stefan has resolved to institute a root-and-branch organizational transformation, which they have called the 'Focus' project. Instead of having the same sales force in each country offering every customer the same product range, the organization will now be built around three market segments: industry, housing developments and individual homes. In each country each segment is to benefit from a customized range with differential pricing and a dedicated sales force. The new structure will help defend market share in price-sensitive segments, whilst boosting quality of service for the more demanding customers – and improving margins.

Stefan puts his organization in place centrally. He summons all the national managers and gives them a presentation about the Focus project. He asks them to restructure their local organizations over the coming weeks. Six months later, things have barely got going. Just two countries have implemented the plan within their own organizations. At a further meeting, Stefan once more explains the need to make changes. He issues thinly veiled threats to replace those national managers who do not act at the earliest possible opportunity. By a year after the launch of Focus, a third country has got its house in order. The other 24 are citing a number of difficulties for inaction.

Stefan feels humiliated: 'They spend more time finding excuses than they do overcoming obstacles.' He has the feeling that he has given his all. 'We have explained things to them. They have heard us. They have understood. In principle, they have accepted the need for this reorganization. Yet nothing happens.' After a pause, he splutters, 'What on earth are they all waiting for?'

We all sometimes find that it is not enough for our people to have heard, understood and accepted a project for it to be implemented. So why do intelligent people drag their feet when they quite clearly need to act?

Sound reasoning is generally enough to ensure that people do not oppose initiatives introduced by others. However, if they are to act themselves, there also needs to be an emotional aspect, a positive desire. If that desire is lacking, it is often for one of four reasons: your people may not feel that they are understood; they may not feel they receive any recognition; they may not associate the project with any positive emotion; or, lastly, their managers' behaviour may remove any desire to take the initiative.

Right, they've understood! Now it's your turn

The less progress is made, the more we become impatient and the less we listen. It's only human. Yet the less we listen, the less we are listened to and the less progress is made.

Stefan's people fully understood the benefits of Focus. They knew that they needed to adapt to trends in competition. They knew that they needed to differentiate between the three major customer segments. Yet they did not feel that they had been understood.

Within Stefan's organization, Peter is responsible for Hungary. The reorganization poses real problems for him. He lacks staff with sufficient skills to lead the three sales forces that are to be set up. He fears that he will lose customers by reallocating portfolios among his sales reps. His salespeople will have to accept a reduction in the scope of their responsibilities to a single type of customer, but with much larger geographic areas and longer journeys. He does not know how to convince them to accept this. Stefan's lectures and warnings do not encourage Peter to act. On the contrary, he feels discouraged. He has a sense that the problems that he faces are not understood and not taken into account. Peter also feels that he is being asked to break up an organization that has worked rather well so far in Hungary. Starting from scratch nine years ago, the team has conquered almost 20 per cent of the market. Of course, that figure is still lower than the group's global market share, but in the particular Hungarian context it is a great performance. He has been in post for five years and feels that Stefan's project is implicitly questioning his personal abilities. The way in which he has organized his teams is deemed inefficient. His approach to the individual housing market is seen as far too unimaginative. His commercial policy towards major deals is thought insufficiently proactive.

Meanwhile, Stefan initially felt that the more he listened to his people, the more they took refuge behind excuses for not implementing Focus. Yet, faced with such resistance, he has now decided to change his approach. So, in the run-up to the latest managers' convention, he is seeking to better identify the major concerns associated with the implementation of Focus at different managerial levels: specific problems encountered or anticipated; other priorities seen as more or less contradictory; potential risks to be taken into account. He takes advantage of conversations and telephone conferences to ask questions. He finds it enormously stressful to hear problems being raised and not to have immediate solutions to offer. Yet he has set himself a rule that he will keep his counsel, ask for clarification and then accurately rephrase the problem. This will ensure that he has fully understood. He also asks some of the people working directly for him to keep their ears to the ground: what is the true cause of concern among residential market salespeople in small countries? Why are manufacturing managers in central Europe so attached to the old-style organization? What is the potential disaster that some are living in fear of? He also collects ideas for potential solutions, including initiatives that some of his people have already undertaken or are ready to launch locally.

When he opens the convention, Stefan does not beat about the bush. He is determined to ensure that Focus is implemented very rapidly in every country, without exception. He restates the anticipated benefits of the project. However, instead of accusing and threatening, as he had done at the previous meeting, he devotes considerable time and effort to showing his people that they have been understood. He explains that he is aware of the great difficulties that all national managers have to overcome and, one by one, he cites the main problems encountered on the ground, without seeking to minimize any of them. After a brief silence, he adds: 'What really struck me about the things that you told me was the energy that you need to generate in order to handle this project in addition to all your everyday business issues.' Without naming them, he refers to certain national managers who are barely getting a wink of sleep, such is the scale of the problems that they have to overcome. Lastly, he announces that a large part of the meeting will be devoted to working together to find a way of addressing those problems. He ends his introductory speech by stressing his belief that the project will be a success.

The convention is just a few minutes old and it is already a triumph. In reality, people do not act automatically once they have understood. They act once they feel that they have been understood. In order to achieve this, it is obviously not enough just to say 'I understand you' or to make vague pronouncements. You really need to take the time to listen, analyse, summarize and then re-express that summary orally for the people concerned.

In certain circumstances, particularly when the situation is very tense or when the number of people to be listened to is too great, it is useful to employ external consultants. They use different professional tools (semi-directive interviews, feedback groups, even online questionnaires) that are not generally very costly and that protect the anonymity of comments. Employees are generally most appreciative of such initiatives: calling on a specialist is evidence of top management's desire to listen to people properly. If well done, the summary constitutes an objective external expression of their perceptions.

So, for your people to take action, it is crucial that they feel that they have been understood. Yet they must also feel that they have been given recognition.

Appreciate they need to be appreciated: they'll appreciate it

As his managers' convention continues, Stefan gives his people star billing. Firstly, he hands over individual and team trophies, including for original criteria such as boldness or fighting spirit. Each award brings an opportunity to boost personal prestige and to get one or more participants to express themselves in front of their colleagues and senior group executives. Each time that he intervenes in order to congratulate an individual it is an entire community (that global region, that occupation or that rank) that feels valued. Secondly, he pays homage to those who have already implemented the Focus project. He asks them to explain to their colleagues the benefits that they have discovered and what they have learned from their experiences, not forgetting the difficulties that they have had to face. These personal accounts really strike a chord with the other participants. Certain managers express their feelings during the plenary session, while others wait for the small-group workshops in order to go into greater detail about their initiatives. Lastly, as we shall see in the next section, all the participants will be called upon to help develop solutions and action plans.

Not only is all this attention useful in highlighting specific issues; it also gives Stefan's people the feeling that they have been given some recognition.

The need to recognize good results is obvious, but the need to recognize skills is equally crucial. You also have to remember to recognize effort: even if the results do not yet match expectations, nothing is more discouraging for those people who have made an effort than to find that this is ignored. Lastly, simply recognizing individuals is important. Thus, just quoting the names of several people present at a meeting and referring to previous discussions with them increase the desire of the entire group to make a positive contribution to the debate. For that matter, there is no need to wait for a major convention to grant recognition: a word or a gesture to an individual or a group in passing is often enough to profoundly change their perceptions and their behaviour.

So your people must feel that they have been understood and given recognition. Yet they must also feel moved.

Minds switched on? Now win their hearts

So that his people can work on potential solutions, Stefan has put them in groups of five around tables in a large room. With the assistance of a consultant, he organizes group work that is designed to provide stimulus. Each table is competing with the others to propose the best specific solutions to the various problems associated with the Focus project, as presented to them. The general tone is cheerful. Events proceed at a quick-fire pace. The rules of the game avoid any sense of repetition, while the senior executives and the consultant play the role of judges and award points to those teams that come up with the best responses. Each time points are awarded, there is applause and cheering. The teams exchange friendly banter interspersed with bursts of laughter. The substance of the most relevant ideas is discussed and, if necessary, Stefan makes additional contributions. All the best ideas from the work session are collected together in a report that will be distributed to all participants.

For the closing session of the day, artistic talents are brought into play. Some teams are asked to produce a large picture on the theme of Focus, by cutting photos or headings out of a pile of magazines. Other participants are to script and perform two sketches: the first showing everything that you should not do when implementing Focus, and the second illustrating the benefits of implementing the project. A third group writes and sings a song about Focus, to the tune of 'Hey Jude!' The various portraits, sketches and songs cause hilarity and stimulate enthusiasm. The whole work session ends with an awards ceremony (awards of greater symbolic than pecuniary value), a photo session, cocktails and a buffet.

For the participants, this is the first time that Focus has been associated with positive emotions. Until now, the project was a byword for pressure and anxiety. They are now raring to go. They want to return to their teams and put it into action.

We all tend to underestimate the emotional dimension to motivation. Too often we believe that arguments alone will bring others on board, but it is a big step from subscribing to an idea rationally to actually putting it into action. This is particularly true where it involves facing up to uncomfortable, difficult or even painful situations.

That is why events are so important to a corporation, when it comes to getting teams to act. Of course, you need to create a positive atmosphere around a project or priority that you want people to support – and you need to do that on a daily basis, not just once a year. An event that is disconnected from working life will have no lasting impact: a few hours of a successful meeting will not offset a year of disastrous mismanagement. Likewise, staging a festive event in the midst of a grave crisis will confuse everyone. It is also true that it is not enough to gather a large number of people together in a hall for them to feel galvanized. For example, watching a series of slides is rarely an exhilarating experience. Yet events perform an essential role if they allow for the generation of strong, positive, collective emotions about a shared ambition.

This need not involve exorbitant expenditure, just some solid preparation, a degree of methodological professionalism (that's what communications agencies are there for) and, above all, the right behaviour by those managers present.

A STIMULATING ATMOSPHERE

ONE DAY I'M GOING TO PRESS THAT
THING, JUST SO THAT SOMETHING
HAPPENS AROUND HERE

Sparkle and be on top of your game

When he talks about the Focus project, Stefan's eyes sparkle. He may be smiling one minute and serious the next, but he is always fully engaged. He is 'on top of his game'. He conveys the strength of his conviction to others.

Would his people be bursting with enthusiasm if their boss seemed racked with anxiety? Would they feel full of confidence if he seemed riddled with doubt? Would they feel like smiling if he was scowling? Would they get stuck in if he was prevaricating?

It is essential that your people feel that they have been understood and have received some recognition. You must also enable them to feel some positive emotions about your project.

However, ultimately, your personal conduct is the most important element of all. It is also the element that you will find the easiest to act upon.

In conclusion to this chapter...

You have got it: after daring to open the box of secrets, capturing everyone's attention, spelling it out to them and moulding opinion, the fifth key to the energy of engagement consists in providing an emotional spark.

Take this book and hand it to a friendly colleague. Ask your colleague to put the following questions to you:

- So, your people have understood, but do they feel that they have been understood?

- Have you taken the time to listen to them properly? Have you been able to listen to their problems without rushing to prescribe solutions?

- Have you publicly recognized how difficult the task is for the people concerned? Have you stood in front of them to list the main obstacles that they may struggle to overcome?

- If necessary, have you employed an external specialist to carry out a fuller listening exercise?

- Recognize it. Do your people feel that they receive recognition?

- Have you done enough to boost the prestige of the best performers?

- How have you demonstrated your genuine recognition of skills?

- In what way have you highlighted and encouraged initial efforts and early (even modest) progress?

- How have you granted individuals true personal recognition?

- Once their minds are switched on, have you won their hearts?

- How have you created positive emotions around your project?

- What everyday initiatives have you taken?

- What events have you organized or taken advantage of in order to generate enthusiasm? How have you achieved this?

- Do you sparkle? Are you on top of your game?

- How do you demonstrate your determination?

- How do you demonstrate your confidence in your ability to succeed?

- How do you demonstrate your enthusiasm about this project?

If your colleague is not convinced by your answers, you still have some work to do. Otherwise, well done! You can move on to the next chapter.

Part 2
The energy of change

Wouldn't it be so much easier if they changed their habits?

A year after the launch of the 'Quality First' project, considerable efforts have been made to get all personnel working towards this priority. Another survey conducted among staff reveals a remarkable level of support: 'Yes, quality is absolutely essential and we must all play our part.' 'It's true that even in my department I know that I have a role to play, if only indirectly.' 'I'm sure that people are prouder working for a company that really wants to stand out from its competitors because of its high quality.' The board has every reason to express its satisfaction.

Unfortunately, another survey, conducted among customers, reveals very different findings. The company's main customer satisfaction and service quality indicators are stagnating, if not declining, compared to last year's, while certain competitors have made striking progress. Staff motivation has not been enough. Furthermore, they are well aware of it: 'We have to accept that this is still a company with a techie culture: we always put the product before the customer and that cannot be changed overnight.' 'We all want to contribute, but in practical terms it is not always clear how we can go about it.' 'Some of us have done really well, but others have found it more difficult.'

Indeed, changing ingrained habits is difficult. By definition, a company culture develops very slowly. Training is costly and not always effective. Lastly, even if certain teams or certain people adopt the methods and patterns of behaviour expected, it is rare for an entire company to be spontaneously inspired to follow their example. Part 2 of this book offers you solutions to better overcome these three obstacles and to instil the energy of change.

Chapter 6 is entitled 'Lift them out of their comfort zone', and it tackles the difficulties that you may encounter in changing instincts and patterns of behaviour long since embedded in organizational practices. Chapter 7, 'Let talent out of the closet', explains how to develop skills in operational terms. Lastly, Chapter 8, 'Make excellence contagious', offers some clues to speeding up the spread of best practices within an organization.

6 Lift them out of their comfort zone

Why isn't the company culture changing, when it urgently needs to?

Nothing is permanent but change.

Heraclitus of Ephesus

Summary

To start our 'Energy of Change' part, let's focus on how to change deeply entrenched behaviours and attitudes. We'll look at how simple changes to physical layout or organizational structure can have a massive impact on behaviour. Once these have been made, lasting change requires your people to change the language they use, the introduction or replacement of regular rituals and the creation of new role models from both within and outside your organization.

Alone in her office, Isabelle puts her head in her hands. She feels that she has done all she can to get her two teams to work together. Yet nothing ever changes. Her hardware department is in charge of developing high-performance hardware. Her software people are no less diligent in developing packages meeting the highest standards in the market and tailored to suit the company's products. Yet the problems have just got worse over the years.

According to the software department, 'the new versions of the software are superb, but they cannot be used yet as insufficient progress has been made with the hardware. This is despite the fact that we have been asking them to develop a new model for months.' Over at the hardware department, they see things quite differently: 'We are developing some fantastic hardware upgrades, but the software is never compatible.' As for their customers, in response to a customer satisfaction survey they stress that the functions offered by competitors are often not available from the product range on offer from Isabelle's teams.

Thus, six months ago, when Isabelle saw senior executives launch a major project branded 'Customers First', she felt inspired. She immediately saw how she could adapt this project to her division. She made numerous attempts to launch initiatives, to explain, to convince, to motivate, to train and to share best practice. In theory, everyone is in agreement. It would even be true to say that many of them would love to move to new ways of working. Yet, in practice, old habits remain firmly ingrained. People just carry on as before and there is no sign of the progress required.

A sociologist friend recently told Isabelle: 'It's the company culture. Culture is stronger than strategy. You will eventually succeed in moving things forward, but it will take time, a long time, not weeks or months; it will take years.'

Isabelle repeats this phrase, shakes her head and wonders. Fieldwork for the next customer satisfaction survey starts in six months' time. 'What on earth are they all waiting for?'

Let's talk culture

Sometimes celebrated as a great asset, sometimes denigrated as creating resistance to change, company culture is a phenomenon that has been widely analysed and debated. The big question for Isabelle is: how can you change a company culture quickly?

Alongside the suggestions made in previous chapters, we can offer you another three important strategies.

Reshuffle the pack to change their hands

Patterns of behaviour are strongly linked to the organizational context within which they are expressed. Therefore changing structures to produce an organization based upon product lines, customer categories or geographical areas revolutionizes the company culture.

There is no such thing as a perfect organization. Oversimple structures can allow certain dimensions to obliterate others: for example, customers sometimes tend to be overlooked in corporations predominantly organized according to product lines. Excessively complex models based upon multidimensional matrices (customers, products, regions, etc) are often cumbersome and confusing when it comes to decision making and business coordination. So do not try to design the perfect organization. Adopt the structures that will quickly alter behaviour in the manner required. Then change the organization again! Corporations such as Microsoft and Dassault Systèmes deliberately change their organizational structures regularly – and successfully.

Naturally, an organization chart is one thing, but true influence is quite another. Ensure that you appoint true leaders to the key new positions that you create. For these posts you will need people with the greatest possible authority and legitimacy within your corporation. Then the ways in which people work will change very rapidly.

Organization can also play a key role in a basic team. For example, entrust the task of implementing your new priority to a key member of your team, rather than seeing it as 'everyone's responsibility'.

That said, you do not always need to modify organizational structures. Indeed, sometimes changing physical layout will be enough to change behaviour and 'culture'. For example, Isabelle could put her hardware managers and software managers who work for the same customers in the same office. Without changing any organizational structures, she will immediately generate different patterns of behaviour. Within a small team of five or six, the mere fact of changing the location of workstations, or even working hours or room layout for weekly meetings, helps to change everyone's habits. Just as retail specialists study the routes that shoppers take through stores, it is possible to develop a 'route map for people and ideas' and to use geographical location to create new instincts.

However, the culture of an organization is not only linked to organizational structures or physical locations. It is also rooted in words.

Stop using old language: change your vocabulary

Terry, the sales and marketing manager of an insurance firm, explains to a consultant: 'We must change the mentality of our sales and marketing executives. As part of our new strategy, we need genuinely proactive managers, who are in touch with customers. But how can we achieve that? For years, these people have spent their time with their noses stuck in their operating reports, looking at numbers. Whatever we tell them, they won't change their ways. That's the company culture.'

The consultant asks: 'Exactly which positions are we talking about here?'

Terry hesitates, realizing the ridiculousness of the situation, and then replies: 'I'm talking about our sales inspectors.'

One of the first things to do, when you want to change the images associated with a particular role, is to change the words used to describe it. Of course, nothing is worse than 'cosmetic' changes: pretending to make a fundamental improvement when, in reality, you are changing only a label. There is nothing like it for promoting cynicism and sarcastic comments. However, when things need to change fundamentally, the names of those things must change too.

CHOICE OF WORDS

I'VE FOLLOWED YOUR ADVICE.
THE NEXT PROJECT IS TO
BE CALLED THE TITANIC!

If the roles of Terry's sales and marketing managers are to change, this must involve changes at different levels, particularly in the definition of responsibilities, objectives, instructions and working tools. Yet there is a risk that even this will not change how these sales inspectors see their professional role. Changing their job title and calling them, for example, 'sales leaders' will help them to develop a new image of their professional role.

At a major consultancy, a management body is responsible for coordinating the allocation of different resources to the main customer projects. This 'Coordination and Arbitration Council' (CAC) has gradually strayed from its initial brief. It takes very few specific decisions and has become the arena for long and often sterile debates, with each party defending its departmental interests and citing the errors committed by others.

Some members of this body then propose that its mission should be redefined: 'To take the decisions necessary in order to ensure that our customers enjoy the best resources possible'. They suggest a different way of working: shorter meetings with specific objectives and a list of decisions immediately distributed to all corporate project managers. The meeting agenda will be drafted quite differently, quoting specific questions, the answers to which will have to be decided upon during the meeting. Furthermore, to ensure that CAC members change the way in which they see their role, this body will become the 'Customer Resources Steering Team' (CRST).

At a medium-sized company specializing in dairy produce, the event of the year is the Annual Executives' Conference. Throughout the morning of the conference and over lunch, the CEO and board members present the results and main achievements for the last financial year and the priorities for the next 12 months. In the hall, the middle managers generally listen attentively – at least for the first 20 minutes. But for them the highlight of the day is break time and lunchtime, which allow them to talk to colleagues whom they have not had the opportunity to meet during the year. The CEO is astonished to find that information presented at the conference finds its way to very few of their people who did not attend. He finds that delegates launch very few specific initiatives in furtherance of that year's main priorities. So he decides to radically change the meeting agenda and format: he allocates more time to initiatives led by middle managers, particularly initiatives that they will shortly undertake. To ensure that every delegate arrives at this meeting with a fresh mindset, he decides to convert the 'Annual Executives' Conference' into 'Strategy Launch Day'.

In order to change things, you also need to change words – but not words alone. You need to change things and words.

Inspire dreams and celebrate new champions

Isabelle wonders how to get her hardware and software departments to cooperate. She feels that she has already done all she can to promote such cooperation. However, the managers of these two departments were not selected for their ability to cooperate. Jason, a young manager in the software department, is a go-getter gifted with an amazing capacity for overcoming obstacles. He is not a great listener, but his energy alone inspires his team to complete increasingly more ambitious development projects. Molly, who heads the hardware department, is known for her thoroughness and her technical expertise. She is no more of a listener than Jason, but she knows how to win respect and she inspires great trust from her team.

In each of these departments, the people tend to resemble their manager. Jason recruits go-getters, while Molly appoints people with a rigorous mindset. At annual meetings, Jason praises his most energetic team members, while Molly lauds those who stick most precisely to the task in hand.

Isabelle realizes that she needs to offer her people new role models. Those role models could come from outside the company. For example, she could organize a meeting with a team from a company (not a competitor) that has succeeded in establishing perfect cooperation between product and service managers. However, initially it is from within her own company that she needs to appoint new 'champions'. So, at her biannual meeting, she could introduce three of her people who have set a good example in interdepartmental cooperation, get them to tell how they achieved this, praise their efforts and explain how they are the perfect incarnation of the new working methods that the company wants to promote at every level.

In order to change an organization's culture, people need to be able to identify with appropriate role models. Too often we do exactly the opposite. For example, we proclaim the importance of cooperation, but we give promotions to 'lone wolves'. We advertise our customer-oriented approach, but we admire those executives who are skilled at in-house office politics. We claim that we want to innovate, but praise managers or staff who are resistant to change.

We must choose our champions well!

Be a guru and introduce new rituals

Charlie is struggling to promote a customer-oriented approach within a department that has always favoured a technical approach to work. At meetings, they generally address a list of technical issues. The working groups set up for projects are usually based around a technical approach. The events that matter to their people involve technical innovations. Charlie realizes that he must bring customers into the way his people think on a daily basis.

Among the factors that contribute to habits within an organization, there is the multitude of rituals that govern the life of its members: the daily morning briefing in the store, the weekly office update, the new product launch, the annual performance review.

So, Charlie sets up a monthly customer review so that they can learn from feedback provided by his department's internal and external customers. In the entrance to their departmental building, he displays a portrait of the Customer of the Month: the photo is unveiled during an informal staff party on the last Friday in every month and each individual is invited to suggest a question to be put to this customer over the following days. For each new project, Charlie now appoints a customer spokesperson from within his team. Twice a year, he publicly awards a certificate to the staff member who has provided the best customer service. These rituals very quickly put the customer at the heart of their concerns.

Company culture is ultimately a fact of life. It is a set of habits, ways of thinking and patterns of behaviour widely shared within an organization and consolidated by years of collective experience. A company culture always has positive aspects that must be identified, recognized, valued, protected and promoted. It also very often has elements that need to be changed. Those elements are not set in stone. It is certainly not impossible to change a company culture. It sometimes requires territorial adjustments, organizational adaptations or quite simply changes in the physical layout of workstations. Very often, new words, new champions and new rituals will be needed. What is always required is that the managers should act as good role models.

In conclusion to this chapter...

You have got it: the first key to the energy of change is to lift them out of their comfort zone.

Take this book and hand it to a person unconnected with your company, perhaps one of your neighbours. Ask this person to put the following questions to you:

- In a few words, can you describe the 'culture' of your company and/or your team?

- What are its positive aspects?

- What are the habits that you would like to change, so as to enable you to implement your new priorities more effectively?

- Does the way in which you are currently organized contribute to those habits?

- What are you going to do to 'reshuffle the pack' to change that organization?

- How can you quite simply change the 'route map' for people and ideas within your working areas?

- What are the words that should be changed so that you can stop using old language and people can develop a new image of their role?

    - Particular job titles?

    - Particular institutional names?

    - The names of particular meetings?

- Who are the champions that your people listen to? How might these champions contribute to certain instincts and habits?

- Which people from outside your organization could you present as role models?

- Which of your people could you present as a good example to others of new behaviour to be adopted?

- What are the rituals that govern the working lives of your people? How might these contribute to certain instincts and habits?

- As a guru, what are the new rituals that you could introduce on a daily, weekly, monthly or annual basis in order to create new habits that will help to ensure that your priorities are put into practice?

If your neighbour is unconvinced by your answers, you still have some work to do. Otherwise, you can move on to the next chapter.

7 Let talent out of the closet

Why training courses achieve nothing, although they cost you a fortune

If you want one year of prosperity, grow grain. If you want 10 years of prosperity, grow trees. If you want 100 years of prosperity, grow people.

Chinese proverb

Summary

Let's look at how to develop, design and roll out training programmes that support the implementation of your strategy. We'll explore why traditional attitudes to training slow down or even damage strategic programmes. We'll examine the factors managers must consider to minimize the need for training and maximize its effectiveness. Finally, we'll look at the components all training programmes must contain to ensure your people have the desire and opportunity to apply the skills and knowledge gained.

'To demonstrate our commitment to these values, we are launching an in-house promotional campaign for all our sites (the posters are shown on the screen). While we're at it, we are setting up a training programme for all middle managers, which should start from September. The training will pay particular attention to annual appraisal interviews, because we're not making sufficient use of them yet and they are key to promoting these values. That's all for the moment. Any questions?'

Standing in front of the screen, remote control in hand, Rob looks questioningly at the other board members. As HR director for this business services company, he is responsible for rolling out the 'Our Values' project, designed to promote and publicize the company's newly defined values to all staff.

'I think that we are really reconnecting with the values that we decided upon at our seminar in the Algarve,' adds Jeremy, the managing director. The board had met in Portugal a few months earlier to work together on several crucial issues. That is how the team defined four essential values designed to drive and characterize the company's thinking: Ambition, Commitment, Loyalty and Solidarity.

Lucy, the sales and marketing manager, offers her view: 'I think that's all very well, but how do you hope to train all our executives when the last quarter of the year is the busiest?'

'Quite so,' replies Rob. 'There's no question of disrupting business activities. That is why we are only training the middle managers and it will then be up to them to promote these values on a regular basis. In addition, for financial reasons, the training programme will be spread over two years. So, every fortnight, I plan to send a group of 10 people on a two-day training course. Part of the training will relate to our values, while the rest will be a refresher on how to conduct annual appraisals.'

Lucy feels reassured. If her arithmetic is correct, over the last quarter just 50 middle managers will be taken away for two day's training – and that should not place too much of a burden on sales.

A few weeks later, a training agency is appointed. It was chosen for its original approach to the subject of values: to get the course members to play with building blocks. The game has been designed so that built-in traps will lead them to a dead end, demonstrating that, if they take no account of their common, shared values, their building blocks project is bound to fail.

The second day of the course deals with annual appraisals. The trainer examines each element of the process: making appointments, preparation, handling the appraisal face to face, using the appraisal as coaching support and drawing useful lessons from the resulting report. The basic rules are highlighted at every stage, and a few role-play games allow them to put certain phases of an appraisal into practice and to identify a few common errors.

Unfortunately, a year after the launch of the first sessions, the assessment is damning: training session evaluation ratings are falling, it has become increasingly difficult to find managers available to attend and there is a huge number of last-minute cancellations. Above and beyond all these setbacks, it has to be said that the training initiative has served almost no purpose. Indeed, there has been no increase in the number of annual appraisals, with the rate stagnant at 60 per cent. Worse still, when people are asked about it, many of them claim to be unfamiliar with the company's values. Others express doubt, if not cynicism, when asked to compare the values being promoted with the conduct actually observed.

Rob has just told his project team that the training programme is to be cancelled. Raising his eyes from his PC, he glances at the 'Our Values' poster pinned to his office wall. 'But, when all's said and done, they are great values,' he thinks to himself. Then he asks aloud, 'What on earth are they all waiting for?'

Everyone loves training. Enormous budgets are squandered on training. In many annual reports, top management proudly boasts about the continuous rise in expenditure under this heading. It should be said that training now fulfils three separate functions:

reinforcing employees' professionalism, updating skills and, importantly, helping to implement strategic initiatives. It is only this last dimension that interests us here. This book does not cover issues relating to the training of top managers or executives.

The problem is that many training courses achieve nothing – and most others serve little purpose. Indeed, in no way does the satisfaction of participants at the end of a session allow you to prejudge the sequel: are they going to put what they have learned into practice? Are they going to change their habits? Are they going to improve performance levels? This is by no means always the case.

So why do intelligent, well-motivated people persist in failing to implement the things that they have learned during training? We shall see how, very often, they are unable to. Sometimes they are also unwilling, or they may be incapable. Lastly, they are sometimes just plain scared.

Shortly we shall see that there are simple means of radically increasing the practical purpose served by training programmes.

They can't do it

Annie is a middle manager at Rob's company. She has gone through the training process. Yet she has not carried out her annual appraisal interviews with her people this year. She explains: 'I had to sign up for the training course three times. On the first two occasions, my boss asked me to postpone my attendance because of various emergencies. During the session, he also asked me to join him at a budget meeting, which meant that I missed the morning of the second day.'

After the course, things did not get any easier: 'I had to talk about the Ambition value at a time when my boss was asking my team to "cool it a bit" at the end of the year, to avoid being set excessively high targets for the next year. In theory, I was supposed to be carrying out end-of-year appraisals, but I had not even had my own appraisal with my boss. Furthermore, I knew that there was a risk that I would not be able to fulfil commitments that I had made. In any case, I attended the training course in February, several weeks after the annual appraisal period had ended.'

If, like Annie, your people are not implementing what they have learned during training, maybe it is because they are unable to do so. This may be because of their working environment: management indifference or hostility towards the content of the training; inadequacy of tools or resources; or insufficient delegation of the authority to act. Alternatively, it may just be poor timing. In Rob's case, certain executives were trained in the company's 'values' more than a year after these had been displayed on all the noticeboards. That was too late, just as it was when Annie attended end-of-year appraisal training in February. In other cases, we seek to provide training for our people for duties to be carried out in the distant future, and that is clearly too early. You merely cause them to lose interest in their current job, while learning skills that they will quickly lose because of a lack of practice. Lastly, the mere fact that different people from the same team receive training several months, or even several years, apart is a grave error. As we have known for more than 60 years, it is difficult, if not impossible, to change your habits in isolation, in an environment that is not changing.[1]

They don't want to do it

If your people do not want to put their training into practice, it is generally because they feel that changing their habits does not bring enough benefits to outweigh the disadvantages. The change required often feels like a bind: more work (initially, at least); new difficulties to cope with; the risk of failure, etc. This all creates a certain degree of discomfort. When the advantages are also unclear – or uninspiring – to the people concerned, they will be tempted to carry on as before. All the preconditions for failure are fully met when their line manager also shows little consideration for the training that people are to undergo. They are placed in an invidious position: either they are 'no good' because they have to attend training that is not highly valued, or they are tempted to show that they have nothing to learn, as the training is considered pointless for them.

They don't know how to do it

Yasmeen has just come back from her training course. For three days she has been examining the rules on matrix management. Her company's new strategy involves a 'two-dimensional' organization: arranged vertically by country and horizontally by product range. Under this new structure, she has quite a distinctive dual role, managing her team locally and adopting a horizontal leadership role supervising the international coordination of quality assurance. Over those three days, Yasmeen was able to get to know her colleagues and finally put a face to the voices that were so familiar over the phone. In addition, the training sessions were lively and the subjects tackled were new and stimulating for her. However, now that she is back in her office, Yasmeen finds it quite difficult to implement new practices. Indeed, as she sees it, the organization within which she works does not really compare with the one used as an example on the course: the methods presented are only applicable on an ad hoc basis. Furthermore, her situation is a bit unusual as she still has a direct management role. Lastly, she sees quality assurance as a distinct function within the company and believes that many of the matrix management rules do not apply to her role. Ultimately, rather than reopen the folder that she was given at the course to see how the contents can be adapted in real life, it just seems easier to continue as before.

Yasmeen's situation is not unusual. People return from training courses feeling satisfied, but they do not change their working methods one iota. What they have learned bears too little resemblance to their particular circumstances, requiring them to adapt to a degree that not everyone is capable of.

They are too scared to do it

'Well, thanks to Mike and Sandra for that tricky exercise. Now, I'd like to ask those watching: in your opinion, why did Mike not succeed in negotiating effectively with Sandra?' At one time or another, we have probably all experienced a situation like this: putting two participants in a difficult situation in front of others and then listing and dissecting the various errors that they have both committed, sometimes with video evidence, a popular method employed during many behavioural training sessions.

Such exercises may allow you to illustrate a number of errors to avoid. However, they symbolize everything that makes people too scared to put what they have learned during training into practice. If they are placed in an awkward situation, people will obviously not feel full of confidence, even if they did previously. Those reduced to the role of observers are even more ill prepared. Did you learn to swim by watching your friends do lengths of the pool?

If we do not have the opportunity to (successfully) implement a method or practice during a course, we will certainly not feel at ease trying to put it into practice in real life. Ultimately, we might wonder whether training really serves any purpose when it comes to getting teams to work towards the implementation of a project.

Based upon our experience of successful projects, here are a few specific proposals to ensure that your training programmes serve as true catalysts for action. If possible, make training courses obsolete. If you need to train people, then train everyone and do it immediately. Develop skills, but also the desire to act. Above all, continue to train people after the course has ended.

Where possible, make training courses obsolete

Fifteen years ago, any change in a basic office software package required in-depth user training within every company. We now switch from one version to the next almost without realizing it. The software publishers do all that they can to make training superfluous. Firstly, they design their new versions to minimize user constraints. Users can mostly work as they did before. Shapes, colours and locations are retained. Secondly, they enable users to obtain an instant online response to any queries about using the tool. There is no longer any need for training, as it is pointless to memorize information that is available instantly on demand. Lastly, they spontaneously offer practical advice, at the specific moment when this may help the user. When you are preparing to produce your first graph using the new version of some software, a message will appear offering you the chance to learn about a new function that will help you.

This just seems like common sense. However, in reality, most projects are run quite differently. For a lot of people, projects mean absorbing numerous complicated changes and information that is hard to access or use. The training will be intense and complex (and therefore impossible to memorize in one go) and it may be given too early or too late. Thus, it is often possible to at least reduce the training required, if not to render it superfluous. Here are three suggestions:

1. When designing your project, at every stage keep the number of changes to be made by each individual to a minimum: ensure that all other professional tasks remain completely unchanged.
2. Make a knowledge base available to your people at their place of work or on their workstations, one that will allow them to access information required immediately. This is the role of so-called employee performance support systems (EPSS) tools.
3. Make sure that your people receive assistance at the precise time when they are carrying a task out for the first time, either through a tool or by having an individual guide them one step at a time. If, despite everything, training remains essential (and this is often the case), there are many ways of ensuring that it is fruitful.

If training is required, train everyone immediately

The training plan that Rob developed, which covers only middle managers and which is spread across two years, is destined to fail from the outset.

When adopting major initiatives, it is often because of budgetary constraints and staff availability that companies opt to train only a proportion of the personnel concerned and to stagger this over several years. These actions are connected to a dated perception of training. In particular, many people believe that it is impossible to provide proper training if a group is too large or a course too short. They are correct, if you confine yourself to traditional training methods. However, it is possible to do things differently.

For example, the authors of this book have often seen how it is possible to cut the duration of training courses for strategic initiatives by over 50 per cent, increase group size from 10 to 60-plus and deliver increased effectiveness.

To achieve this, firstly you need to define your training objectives very precisely. What are the two or three key messages that are essential for your people to understand? What are the few details that they really must know by heart? Above all, though, what exactly must they do – and in which particular situations? During the preparatory phase, we must limit the number of topics to be addressed during a course. In practice, we tend to overestimate the amount of information that our people really need to know, so that presentations become very tedious and only a small (and random) proportion of the information is remembered. In contrast, we tend to underestimate the difficulty of adopting new habits, which is why an insufficient proportion of training is hands-on.

It is also essential to adopt innovative educational methods. Blended learning, which combines online self-tuition with experience-sharing sessions and classroom training, is one example of this.[2] More specifically, there are training methods to suit large groups that concentrate on getting people to work individually or in pairs. To limit the time taken by training, particularly in 'white-collar' occupations, it is also possible to arrange for real work to be completed during sessions. For example, in order to practise a method of preparing for visits, salespeople can establish negotiating objectives for real customers. Lastly, the timing of training is important: if the training comes too long before implementation, it is relatively ineffective. If it comes too late, that is worse. You need to train on a just-in-time basis.

Overall, experience proves that it is always possible to train all the people involved in a strategic initiative at the right time and at a very reasonable cost, provided that you adopt very specific objectives, concentrate the training within a short period and employ suitable methods.

However, you have to go beyond training courses, to provide your people with proper practice.

Teach less, train more

On completion of a training course, many people find it hard to put the learning into practice.

This may initially be due to the over-general nature of the content, which requires participants to transpose the course contents to the various issues that they have to deal with. Yet, unlike top managers and executives, who have been educated to be comfortable with the idea of juggling concepts and transposing ideas from one context to another, most staff members are quite ill prepared for this. Some express this forcibly: 'That's all well and good. It may work in theory, but real life isn't like that.' Others may initially be seduced by the course contents, but then discover that they do not always know how to apply them in practice. Therefore, if training needs to be transferred to everyday tasks, this should be done by the course designers before the course and not by the participants afterwards.

The second reason relates to inadequate practical training. In reality, only repeated, targeted practice allows people to gain both the self-confidence and the instincts essential to the effective implementation of new habits.[3] So your people must do particular practical exercises that are fully representative of the work that they do. Still better, it could involve real situations that they will have to deal with. Ideally, training should be carried out on the job, eg in the warehouse or workshop.

Ignite a spark

We usually take the view that training is designed to develop skills, that is to say expertise. This often involves 'know-what' and 'know-how'. Yet, while the possession of highly skilled personnel is certainly a precious asset, in no way does it guarantee an active commitment to a new priority: aside from reinforcing skills, these days training must also ensure that each of your people has a desire to act. There are three essential components to this: meaning, confidence and enjoyment.

Providing meaning requires you to connect every effort required (the discomfort involved in acquiring a new 'habit' or changing patterns of behaviour) to a purpose that makes it worthwhile. This purpose may serve the interests of customers, the company or even the individual concerned. Taking the example of training for annual appraisals, it is interesting to find out how reports are used subsequently. By making our individual contribution part of a more general initiative, we get the feeling that we are contributing to something useful, something meaningful.

As human beings, we also need to feel confident if we are to face up to new situations – or to face up to acting differently in familiar situations – so it is essential that each person should be enabled to succeed during a training programme. In particular, practical exercises must be simple and must be repeated as often as necessary until the new 'habit' has been learned.

Lastly, the enjoyment factor is also very important. We take pleasure in doing what we enjoyed learning. But how can we enjoy training? Can we really associate enjoyment with something as serious as training for a strategic business project? The good news is that we can, and there are several ways of doing so.

The first consists in creating group dynamics. Training managers and staff in groups of 30 or 50 allows you to adopt new organizational methods that use the dynamism created by working in large groups. Contrary to what many people believe, large-group training and intensive training are not mutually exclusive. For example, it is possible to organize team-based tournaments that revolve around resolving particular problems. Where they are well controlled by the trainer, friendly competitions around operational topics allow people simultaneously to develop their skills, exchange best practice and generate enthusiasm, even about a subject initially perceived as difficult.

Another key factor is to help each person to use their particular personal strengths to contribute to a project, because we all take pleasure in carrying out tasks for which we feel that we possess a particular talent. To achieve this, the debriefing for each exercise needs to be designed to allow each individual to identify the main strength that they have just used. Thus, during future training the participant will rely on this strength even more and do even better.

Naturally, the choice of trainer is crucial. The trainer's capacity to provide participants with meaning, confidence and enjoyment is decisive to the effectiveness of a training programme. The trainer's teaching ability and particularly their personality count at least as much as their technical expertise.

Plan for the future now

It is after the training session that the work really begins. In fact, the main reason why training courses fail is the indifference of middle management. When staff members are confronted for the first time with a situation requiring a new way of working, are they encouraged, supervised, assisted and, if appropriate, congratulated? Do their line managers lead by example, in the way that they handle similar situations?

It is true that certain old management maxims need to be brought into question. However, among those that must not be changed is the need to always start by training the organization's top managers and then train middle managers before moving on to the lower echelons. Thus, each manager explains the training objectives to their people and then works with each of them to identify particular skills to be acquired during the session. Then, after the training has ended, the manager can give each person effective support to put that training into practice. This managerial support must form part of the training initiative. Aside from the teaching materials used for the participant, the manager must also be given specific resources for this, eg a support guide, a tool facilitating work monitoring or a document allowing refresher sessions to be staged at meetings.

In conclusion to this chapter...

You have got it: after lifting them out of their comfort zone, the second key to promoting the energy of change is to let talent out of the closet.

Take this book and hand it to a schoolteacher. Ask the teacher to put the following questions to you:

● Have you done all you can to make training obsolete?

● At every stage of your project, have you sought to limit the number of habits that the different people involved have to change?

● Have you provided your people with a knowledge base allowing them instant access to information required at their workplace or from their workstation?

● Have you ensured that your people receive assistance from a tool or an individual providing step-by-step guidance at the precise time when they carry out a task for the first time?

● Have you done all you can to train everyone immediately?

● Have you defined the training objectives very precisely?

　– The two or three simple messages that your people must remember.

　– Those few items of information that they must learn by heart.

　– The actions and behaviour required in a few specific and well-defined situations.

● Have you employed innovative teaching methods to train larger groups in less time?

- Have you ensured that part of the training time will be devoted to carrying out real work?

- Have you checked that each of your people was trained on a just-in-time basis?

- Have you taught little and trained a lot?

- Is the training tailored very specifically to the main situations that your people encounter?

- Is the bulk of the programme devoted to focused practice?

- Is that training based upon real circumstances that the participants deal with? Is it carried out on the job?

- Have you ignited a spark and lit their desire to act as well as developing their skills?

- Have you given meaning to the work required, by connecting it to worthwhile outcomes?

- Have you boosted your people's confidence by putting each of them in a situation where they can succeed via simple, repeated exercises?

- Have your people taken pleasure from getting trained?

- Have you used the dynamism particular to large groups?

- Have you given each of them an opportunity to put their personal strengths to specific use?

- Have you appointed enthusiastic trainers who are good teachers?

- Have you planned for the future?

- Have your middle managers been trained after top management but before your staff?

- Has specific provision been made for middle managers to prepare for the training of all staff members and to then support them when they put what they have learned into practice?

- Have you equipped your middle managers with the tools required to ensure that they can play their role in promoting training?

If the schoolteacher is unconvinced by your answers, you still have some work to do. Otherwise, move on to the next chapter.

Notes

1. See, *inter alia*, the works on change by Kurt Zadek Lewin (1890–1947).
2. A more precise definition of blended learning is available from the Training and Blended Learning page of the website www.korda-partners.com, together with some examples of teaching methods.
3. In his book *Talent Is Overrated* (Portfolio, New York, 2008), Geoff Colvin demonstrates that only practice allows people to achieve high performance levels. See also *The Road to Excellence* (Lawrence Erlbaum Associates, Mahwah, NJ, 1996), which presents the research of Professor K Anders Ericsson, a leading light in this field.

8 Make excellence contagious

Why can't they all match the top performers, when all they have to do is to copy?

It is by copying that we invent.

Paul Valéry

Summary

Now we'll discover the keys to making the performance of your best people contagious across the business. We'll demonstrate how to design and roll out best practice sharing so that it is enthusiastically applied by as many of your people as possible. We'll finish with examples on how to embed these best practices so that they seamlessly blend into business operations.

Luke manages a network of bank branches. One of his main objectives is to boost sales of insurance products, as their market share has taken a hit. His 'Insurance Is a Core Business' project is a priority for the bank.

For years now Luke's branches have been offering their customers insurance solutions for their homes, cars and health. However, most of their people still find it hard to sell products that customers do not naturally ask their bankers to provide. That is why Luke has adopted various measures in this area. He started by ensuring that the 'Insurance Is a Core Business' project was fully understood and accepted and even generated enthusiasm. Then he launched various initiatives designed to change the culture of his network from that of a traditional banking business to 'banking and insurance': new organization, new words, new champions and new rituals – nothing was overlooked. He has also organized several major training programmes on this subject.

So far, none of this has produced acceptable results. The overall figures are still disappointing. This applies to every region and every product range. However, taking a closer look at the figures, Luke notices two interesting phenomena.

Firstly, on average some branches achieve an insurance supply ratio of almost two (each customer has two insurance policies with the bank), whereas the average is less than half a product per customer. Luke's team has tried to identify characteristics that might distinguish high-performing branch results from the mediocre results achieved by the rest. They tried in vain. Competitive pressures are comparable, customer profiles are no different and the profiles of personal advisers are similar.

Secondly, within a single branch there are considerable performance disparities between different personal advisers: some sell three products per customer, others hardly any. Once again, Luke's team has tried to identify structural factors that might explain this. Did those who are best at selling insurance products previously work in insurance? No. Do they have a different customer portfolio from the others? No. Have they received training, tools or support unavailable to others? They have not.

It is by personal research on the ground that Luke becomes aware of the reasons for these performance disparities. It is not a question of the competition or the customers, but a question of habits. For example, at one medium-size suburban branch, when a customer asks for credit to buy a car, the adviser is in the habit of immediately offering to take care of the car insurance. When a customer carries out an unusual (credit or deposit) transaction, the adviser is in the habit of suggesting a customer review, covering the issue of insurance amongst others.

When he presents his impressions to his team at HQ, Luke expresses his confusion. 'It is so simple that anyone could do it. All they need to do is to follow the example set by the top performers,' he sighs, 'and I'm sure they covered all this during their training.' One of his people interjects: 'What on earth are they all waiting for?'

Luke's problem may seem particularly discouraging, as it reminds us all of the difficulties that we have faced in ensuring that good habits are adopted consistently throughout our organization.

Performance disparities may result from external causes associated with the market or the economic climate. Sometimes particular individuals may also possess an exceptional, almost instinctive, talent that explains their extraordinary levels of performance. Yet, in many cases, all that is required to rapidly improve performance levels is for most staff members to adopt the habits of the top performers in their midst. Why do they not do so? Why do intelligent people facing problems on a daily basis not successfully employ solutions that are within reach? Maybe it is because they do not really know what the top performers do. No doubt that is because they have never really been encouraged to draw inspiration from them.

So you need to identify the habits of your top performers and ensure that others adopt those habits. Then you need to encourage them to put those habits into practice.

Be a meddler and identify the habits of top performers

In principle, everyone is in agreement: it would be great to know how those who are the best at resolving our common problems manage it. Yet teams are located in different countries, on different sites or quite simply on different floors or in different offices. There are often severe time constraints. Meetings are short and agendas packed to overflowing. They are mainly devoted to firefighting, not to discussing what works well and could be applied universally. That is why many companies launch into projects designed to identify best practices.

Naturally, one working method consists in looking outside the company, at the practices employed by other high-performing companies. This is known as benchmarking.[1]

When carried out within a particular industry, benchmarking does not yield a crucial advantage, but it can help a company to keep up with its top-performing rivals. However, when carried out beyond the boundaries of a business sector, it can allow a corporation to import and adapt ideas that will be true innovations in their new context. Yet the quickest and safest means of ensuring that a group of people achieves progress is to share what already works within that group.

Richard Tanner Pascale and Jerry Sternin, two American academics, have conducted research into this issue.[2] Their studies have addressed issues as varied as changes in commercial methods at a bank and the struggle against excessive school dropout rates in Argentina. This research has shown that resistance to change within a community can often be overcome much more easily where the innovators are members of that community. So, within a particular group, you need to identify 'positive deviants': individuals who, with the same constraints and resources as the others, are employing different practices and achieving better results.

The search for best practices within a company has three other very important benefits. Firstly, the practices that are selected have already proven their worth. This allows you to avoid the cost and delays associated with the development or testing phases often necessary when introducing new practices within an organization. Secondly, those practices are inherently suited to the company's circumstances, thereby removing the objection that you usually hear from your people: 'Yes, that works well elsewhere, but things are very different here.' Lastly, that search constitutes a great way of giving recognition to those who have been able to adapt and introduce successful practices.

Yet collecting best practices within an organization is not particularly easy. Two traps lie in wait for you.

The first misplaced brainwave is wanting to collect the ideas of all your people, as 'Deep down, everyone has good ideas.' Your intentions are noble, and this approach will boost everyone's morale. However, you risk ending up with a mishmash of successful and unsuccessful practices, sometimes making the cure worse than the disease. The other disadvantage is the glut of information, which generally leaves staff perplexed: 'Where do we start?'

The second misplaced brainwave is identifying the practices of those teams or people posting the best results in absolute terms, for example the best profit margins. Once more, your intentions are good, but in truth the best performances in absolute terms are often the result of long-standing experience rather than good practices.

The best way of identifying best practice is therefore to identify the practices that set those teams or individuals making the most progress apart from the rest, perhaps over the last two years. In reality, those making the best progress have almost always introduced effective practices that can easily be replicated.

Once best practice has been identified, you must do some sorting. In reality, not all the ideas that you collect will necessarily be transferable. Some will be difficult to put into practice; others will be too costly. So you should retain only those practices that are the most relevant and the easiest to deploy throughout the organization, to achieve rapid results.

You must then formalize those practices. Each idea must be recorded on a card containing a title, a few lines of procedures (like a recipe card), the advantages of the method, the precautions to be adopted... and the name of the inventor. Crediting the inventor is an important act of recognition. It also allows you to promote direct discussion between peers.

Once this work is done, you will have a true treasure trove. Many top managers merely place this at the disposal of their teams, who can consult the best practices according to their needs. Unfortunately, this is ineffective. The hard work has yet to be done.

Don't be prescriptive: offer them options from a menu

Ultimately, there are three ways of encouraging your people to adopt new habits.

Your first option is to set high targets ('what to do') but to leave your people to choose the means used ('how to do it'). This is target-based management. 'Here are the results that you must achieve: reduce the number of quality anomalies by 10 per cent, improve customer satisfaction by three points, increase productivity by five points, etc.' Your teams must find solutions either by innovating or by spontaneously discovering and adopting the best practices introduced by others.

The second option is to dictate both 'what to do' and 'how to do it'. This is process-based management, as top managers describe it – or procedure-based management, as their people often see it. Within small and medium-sized businesses processes are often insufficiently formalized. In contrast, within large corporations, staff members are often already hemmed in by rules and constraints of every sort. So making best practices compulsory does not always produce very good results, as each new rule arouses fierce resistance: 'This does not suit my circumstances'; 'Yet another senior management idea: you can see that they haven't been on the front line for ages'; 'That will not work within our department.' Ultimately, the orders given are not always implemented with intelligence and goodwill.

The third option, and our recommendation, draws its inspiration from Chinese restaurant menus, which offer a broad range of options with numbers attached. It involves offering a choice about 'how to do it' and allowing each individual to select the practices best suited to their particular circumstances.

Thus, a long time ago Southwest Airlines, which is famed for the quality of its in-flight service, identified the various practices allowing the cabin crew to provide passengers with an incomparable 'customer experience'.[3] However, those practices are not imposed. On each airliner the flight attendants possess a Fun Book, which lists all sorts of initiatives that have proven successful. Depending upon their individual personality, their mood on the day and the atmosphere that they perceive on board, they can select those ideas that seem to be the best suited to making the passengers' trip more enjoyable.

More specifically, in order to help your colleagues or your people to draw up suitable progress plans, you can offer them a short working session at one of your team meetings. The objective is to reveal best practices (identified and formalized in advance) and to select those that would be the most useful in their circumstances.

The participants begin by classifying the best practices into four categories. Firstly, there are those that can be classified as an area of excellence: 'We understand and use this so well that we no longer even think about it.' Then there are the strengths: 'We apply this quite well and fairly systematically.' Next come the weaknesses: 'We do not apply this very well or very systematically.' Lastly, there are the still unknown practices: 'We have never thought of this' or 'We have never really tried this.'

Then the team identifies the most beneficial practice from each category. It is then easy to focus on a few instant initiatives that will allow significant progress to be made: a 'still unknown' one for experimentation, a weakness to be corrected, a strength to be further reinforced and an area of excellence to be further exploited. Ideally, you should set a few priorities collectively, and each individual should also choose one or two additional practices for personal implementation.

This approach may be deployed within a large organization. For example, over the past few years the authors have led projects in which a few dozen members of a corporation, trained in less than two hours, have gone on to organize meetings for thousands of people within a few weeks, thereby generating an abundance of initiatives and spectacular progress in the areas addressed.

EXCELLENCE CAN BE

CONTAGIOUS

CAN YOU EXPLAIN TO ME
WHY YOUR FLOOR HAS NOT
BEEN CONTAMINATED?

Adopt the toothbrush strategy: no debate, just daily application

Adopting a new habit always requires effort. Persisting in it requires none. Hopefully, we all experienced this when we acquired the habit of brushing our teeth every day. Various studies demonstrate that top sports champions stand out through their ability to adopt and incorporate certain habits both in training and in competition. It is by making a practice systematic, regular and identical (we refer to routine or even ritual) that we acquire a habit. It then becomes a mere instinct and no longer requires any effort. The British philosopher and mathematician AN Whitehead (1861–1947) observed this as early as 1911: '[Some say] that we should cultivate the habit of thinking of what we are doing. The precise opposite is the case. Civilization advances by extending the number of important operations which we can perform without thinking about them.'[4]

When your people have selected a good practice, it is therefore essential to encourage or even to monitor its immediate daily implementation. One of your main motivational powers is to measure the progress made by the different teams or individuals concerned as frequently as possible, to encourage all of them to continue to apply their new habits. After a few weeks, the instincts will be ingrained and you will be able to concentrate on finding new ways of making progress.

In short, it is perfectly possible to encourage your people to adopt the habits of the top performers in their midst. This type of approach allows you to achieve rapid results with limited resources, since these practices have already proven their worth in-house. It also allows you to improve skills levels and to motivate and give recognition to those who are making progress.

In conclusion to this chapter...

You have got it: after lifting them out of their comfort zone and letting talent out of the closet , the third key to the energy of change is making excellence contagious.

Take this book and hand it to one of your front-line staff. Ask them to put the following questions to you:

- Have you 'meddled in our business' by identifying how our top performers operate?

- Have you really selected the best practices by watching those of us who are making the best progress?

- Have you sorted and then formalized those ideas so as to make them fully usable?

- Have you also identified how they operate at other top-performing companies in other business sectors?

- Instead of being prescriptive, have you offered us options from a menu to ensure that we acquire good habits?

- Have you resisted the desire to impose additional rules and constraints upon us?

- Have you given us the opportunity to consider a range of good practices so as to choose those that would be the most useful to each of us, depending upon our particular circumstances?

- Have you arranged for those practices to be deployed throughout the organization? Has each of my colleagues been able to get involved?

- Have you adopted the toothbrush strategy and encouraged the implementation of those practices?

- Are your people supervised and encouraged every day for the first few weeks?

- Do you frequently and systematically measure the progress achieved?

If your staff member is unconvinced by your answers, you still have some work to do. Otherwise, move on to the next chapter and start reading the final part of this book.

Notes

1. For example, see the international studies carried out by the Leaders for Excellence Forum, a club run by our consultancy, Korda & Partners: www.leadersforexcellence.com.
2. See, *inter alia,* their excellent article 'Your company's secret change agents' in *Harvard Business Review,* May 2005.
3. This remarkable corporation has already been the subject of several interesting books, including *The Southwest Airlines Way* by Jody Hoffer Gittell (McGraw-Hill, New York, 2003) and *Do the Right Thing* by James Parker (Wharton School Publishing, Philadelphia, PA, 2007).
4. AN Whitehead (1911) *An Introduction to Mathematics,* Williams & Norgate, London.

Part 3
The energy of management

What if your middle managers actually served some purpose?

A great deal has now been done in order to ensure that the 'Quality First' strategy is implemented on the ground. During the first year, the entire workforce was mobilized to promote a high quality of customer service. The next year was devoted to training, to sharing best practice and to various initiatives designed to change the company culture. After two years, a customer satisfaction survey finally reveals the first signs of progress. The board sees this as validation of its strategy and a reward for its perseverance. Unfortunately, six months later, in some regions the indicators are already in decline. A year later, the downward trend has afflicted the entire company, although no external cause has been identified.

A further staff survey is carried out, employing very specific questions: 'Did your line manager discuss "Quality First" with you at your annual appraisal interview? At your last team meeting? Over the past six months?' The responses are worrying. Middle management have not actively supported the project. The quality of the people is not at issue: these middle managers were all recently assessed by a prestigious outside consultancy, which was impressed by their skills and their desire to perform well. Yet these managers have not successfully promoted the strategy. They have not always seen 'Quality First' as a priority. They have not taken ownership of their customer satisfaction targets, often considering them to be too high. In truth, the board is not entirely surprised. In other areas, the same phenomena have been identified within the company. Many decisions have not been implemented, despite the universal goodwill.

Part 3 of this book addresses these crucial issues, which all concern the energy of management, that is to say the capacity of middle management to initiate, to orientate, to accelerate and to encourage action within your company.

Chapter 9 is entitled 'Treat your middle managers like VIPs'. It argues for middle managers to be more highly regarded and suggests a few ways of using this to promote your strategy. Chapter 10, 'Pinpoint the target', explains how to mobilize your middle management behind the real priorities. Chapter 11, 'Compare progress', gives you the tools to dismantle one of the most common traps in the 'management of middle managers'. Lastly, Chapter 12, 'Make execution your trademark', invites you to make action your consistent code of conduct, for you personally and for those around you.

9 Treat your middle managers like VIPs

Finally, find out why your middle managers are not passing on the message, since that's what they're paid to do

Every prince needs allies, and the bigger the responsibilities, the more allies he needs.

Machiavelli

Summary

Firstly, we consider why being a middle manager is often undervalued and why middle managers' perspectives are ignored. We'll look at how to engage, involve and gain their support. We then show you how to provide them with a clear plan of action using practical tools. Finally, we demonstrate how to develop and deploy project ambassadors to act as the champions in your business.

The atmosphere in the boardroom is tense. The CEO asks each board member about the progress of ongoing projects.

James, sales and marketing director, coughs nervously: 'Our "Winning Back Customers" plan is just getting going. It's a bit early to talk about results, but we now see clearly how best to move forward and adapt to some of the practical constraints we are facing.' Controlling his irritation, the CEO questions further: 'A bit early to talk about results? Just starting to see things clearly? Remind me, James, just how long have we been discussing this plan?' Stung by the criticism, James retorts, 'Well, hold on a minute, my teams and I are working 15-hour days promoting this plan. Have you any concept of how difficult it is to get new ideas through the layers of middle management and then on to the shop floor? It's taking time, but we're getting there. I'll give you all a detailed update at our meeting on the 15th.'

The CEO sighs and turns to Hannah, the human resources director. 'So how is our mobilization plan going?' Hannah has prepared her contribution: 'I would remind everyone that we are facing a strategic challenge. Within two years we need to arrange for a fifth of our workforce to be redeployed on to our most profitable work. This involves skills reviews, assessment of potential, training plans...' The CEO interrupts her: 'Yes, thank you, Hannah, we are well aware of that. Where are we at the moment?' Hannah responds brusquely, 'I was just coming to that.' Then, turning to her colleagues: 'We are well behind schedule, and the reason for this is the lack of support from the middle managers in the various teams. At some sites we have, shall we say, difficult relations with our trade unions. Some of the unions are taking advantage of our people's anxiety and lack of understanding. As I have already made clear, it is essential that line management should do more to explain just what we are doing.'

Several voices are raised in protest and for a moment confusion breaks out. However, the CEO quickly calls the meeting to order again. 'Let's talk about the quality project. How's that going, Bernie?' Bernie is caught on the hop. 'We are a little behind schedule, to be honest. We have worked really hard to ensure that our middle managers are well informed and fully trained, but it seems as if it is not filtering down. I carried out some research to analyse what the obstacles might be.' The CEO explodes: 'Research? Analysis? A survey about your analysis and your research? What next? I'm getting increasingly concerned that middle managers are not passing on your decisions. You are the ones in charge. You must take responsibility for your decisions. You must ensure that they are implemented. That's what your middle managers are paid for. And these are pretty intelligent people, don't forget!' He stops for a moment, sighs and then vents his exasperation: 'Dammit, what on earth are they waiting for?'

Why, then, do intelligent people with managerial responsibilities not pass company decisions on to their teams? When it is we who are involved, we generally have cast-iron excuses: 'Too much to do'; 'Not enough time'; 'I have other priorities.' With others, we are much more ruthless: 'They're selfish and don't really care about their colleagues or the company.' 'They don't show willing.' 'They never keep their promises.'

Middle management: one of the worst jobs in the world

Fifteen years ago, many highly qualified clerical workers dreamed of achieving middle management status. Better pay, benefits in kind, more interesting work, a prestigious position: there was no shortage of reasons. Today, it has often become difficult for human resources managers to convince their staff to take on a management role.

Firstly, in practice, middle management jobs have lost their attraction. Within ever more process-driven major corporations, middle managers' general room for manoeuvre has been reduced in favour of rules and procedures. Within small and medium-sized enterprises, whose bosses often find it hard to delegate, the management chain is often little more than an information conveyor belt.

Secondly, employees appointed to a management position are subject to numerous constraints: increased stress associated with their responsibilities, longer working hours, the obligation to take responsibility for unpopular decisions that they did not have a part in formulating, and exposure to conflict with staff dissatisfied with their pay or career development. These constraints are generally only marginally offset by higher pay, particularly once account is taken of the shift to a higher income tax bracket.

Not only that, middle management is often held in low esteem by senior managers. Who can remember a great triumph attributed to middle management? No, it never happens. Most often the great triumphs are achieved by enlightened senior executives – or talented and devoted staff. In contrast, middle management is responsible for almost every disaster. If a measure meets workforce opposition, that is the fault of middle management for failing to explain it properly. If feet are dragged over the implementation of a project, it is because middle managers were unable to change their habits. If results are not as anticipated, the finger yet again points at middle managers, who are clearly not up to the job!

In addition, although middle managers are burdened with heavy responsibilities, they usually enjoy none of the benefits accruing to senior managers. Stock options, certain benefits in kind, access to strategic information: none of these are open to them. They are generally treated like just another cog in the wheel.

Lastly, when restructuring is planned with a view to cost cutting, middle management is in the front line for major cutbacks: perceived as underachieving dead wood, middle management layers are the perfect target for major staffing reductions.

Ultimately, you might wonder if a middle management job is not the worst possible job to have within an organization.

But what if you really need them?

Are you a middle manager? You play several crucially important roles.

Naturally, your primary responsibility is team leadership: to assign objectives, to distribute tasks, to motivate, to assist and to check that work is being carried out properly on an everyday basis. This organizational role allows you to tell your senior managers what people are saying on the shop floor.

From contact with teams and often with customers, you will be aware of practical difficulties that are encountered, initiatives that work or changes in the local environment. You are an invaluable source of information and ideas feeding into decisions taken at higher levels within the organization. You are also called upon to play a coaching role, so as to develop your people's skills on an everyday basis. You are ever more required to promote cooperation and horizontal management through networking and project work.

Above all, however, you pass your senior managers' messages and objectives on to front-line staff, thereby reducing your bosses' workload. You need to 'filter' the mass of information that you receive, because you cannot pass all of it on without nuance or explanation. You have to select the information that is relevant, significant and useful. Above all, you have to transform how much and what into why and how. In particular, when you tell your people about a senior management priority, you have to give it some meaning by explaining the reasons behind the work required. You then need to indicate specifically how to go about it so as to achieve the objectives required. We should add that, in general, you will have to simultaneously break down and introduce numerous directives, issued by different functional and operational departments.

So, within all companies, considerable expectations are placed upon you. They cannot do without you. All those who have tried have failed. Middle managers are back!

Is it humanly possible for you who recklessly accepted such responsibilities to satisfy such expectations? The truth is that you cannot – unless you are given a bit of help.

Make them feel special: build a community

The CEO responds to Hannah, the human resources director, regarding the implementation of her mobilization project: 'In your opinion, Hannah, why are middle managers not making this a priority? Could it be a lack of information?'

'Absolutely not,' Hannah protests. 'It's all on the intranet. All they need to do to find out about it is to log on, like any other employees.'

As senior managers, we claim to expect a great sense of responsibility from our middle managers, as well as fierce loyalty to company priorities and an unfailing desire to promote projects. Yet how many of us really treat them as people who have been given a special mission? Too often, middle managers are informed of major decisions at the same time as their people. There is no advance consultation, no particular guidance about their role as intermediaries, no account taken of potential difficulties affecting practical implementation, no message of encouragement and no period within which to prepare for questions from their people – nothing.

Yet some companies do succeed in creating a true community of middle managers. For example, one of the authors of this book, who previously held a senior management position at a service company, informed his 50 middle managers (divisional bosses, departmental managers and major account executives) that he saw them as members of a 'club'. Membership of that club had its benefits. Within 24 hours of each senior management meeting ending, club members would receive an exclusive summary of the main decisions taken. Each quarter, a three-hour meeting was devoted to a training session, to sharing experiences or to meeting a senior manager or leading figure from outside. Club members enjoyed complete freedom of expression at their meetings; no subject was taboo. Lastly, they all knew that senior management would stand up for them (publicly, at least) in the event of a dispute with another employee. However, club membership also imposed certain duties. Solidarity between members was one golden rule. In the event of a dispute between staff from their respective teams, middle managers would have to adopt a conciliatory approach and handle the matter in private. Above all, though, once a management issue had been debated, with each person having freely expressed their opinion, everyone had to support the decision taken.

This approach proved spectacularly effective, particularly on the eve of a tricky restructuring project. Three days before the decisions were announced to all personnel, the club members all met. Organized in subgroups, the members worked on sensitive issues: what were the main benefits of restructuring that should be highlighted for our people? What were the main disadvantages in the eyes of the different groups concerned? How could each of those disadvantages be limited? What further improvements could we make to the project or to how it was implemented? Each subgroup provided direct and sometimes forceful feedback about its conclusions. After a brief discussion with those in attendance, the senior management team immediately pronounced judgement by classifying each proposal in one of the following three categories: accepted, rejected or, on an exceptional basis, placed on the agenda of the next meeting for in-depth discussion and decision. The meeting ended with a review of the decisions taken and the messages to be promoted. Participants were thanked for their contributions, many of which facilitated further improvements to decision making. Each individual was called upon to help make the announcement a success, by personally informing those people who were the most directly affected by changes. Three days later, contrary to many predictions, the restructuring announcement was given a very good reception.

While executives and members of middle management have duties, they also have rights. As senior managers, if you want their support, you must treat them as important members of your organization, in a class of their own. You must inform them in advance. You must listen to them and involve them in choosing solutions. Of course, you must also encourage them.

Once you have won their support, you must then help them to put things into practice.

Go by the stars if you wish, but make sure you give your middle managers a GPS

The CEO turns to Bernie, the quality director, again. 'I don't understand why things are taking so long. You did distribute the outline of our new processes, the new quality indicators and the new control and audit procedures to all staff, didn't you?'

'Yes,' confirms Bernie. 'They have all the information. All they need to do is to translate it into language that their teams will understand and to arrange to comply with it. Nothing too complicated!'

The problem is that something that constitutes an objective for a senior manager can sometimes become a burden for a middle manager. Something that is a specific daily concern for the former often becomes an unexpected and abstract issue for the latter. Something that constitutes an absolute priority for one becomes, for the other, yet another problem to be dealt with amongst dozens of others.

When you are a senior manager, responsible for an important issue, it is sometimes hard to imagine just how difficult it can be for middle managers to grasp that issue and to arrange for its effective implementation by their teams. That is why it is important to provide your middle management with specific practical assistance in implementing decisions.

Some people find their way using a compass; some are simply guided by the stars. A far greater number reach their goal more safely with the aid of a GPS navigation system. In order to help your middle managers find their way, simple 'communications kits' featuring slides are a great start. These can often be made more user-friendly if they allow significant scope for interactivity: 'How does this apply to our team? Who can give an example of something we do that relates to this? Which of our team's methods should be retained and which should be changed if we are to comply with this new rule?' For example, when faced with strategic objectives, it is crucially important that each team should take the time to understand how its work helps to achieve each of the organization's goals.

It may be very useful for such kits to be complemented by practical tools allowing middle managers to assess their team's situation, to select specific initiatives to be adopted locally and to monitor their progress. However, the profusion of tools (often distributed in documentary format, without any open discussion) sometimes leaves middle managers powerless: in practice, you need to provide them with support, for example in the form of implementation leaders. For example, during a brand change at a major telecoms operator, the senior management used 'brand ambassadors' on each site to help middle managers inform and mobilize their teams and to take the measures required in every sphere.

Make fewer enemies and more allies

Middle management must constitute the nexus of a network of allies working to implement your priority.

Within a small business or institution, it is quite easy to consult all middle managers about major decisions and to bring them on board. Within a large organization, it is obviously impossible. However, experience shows that much can be done in order to get middle management more involved at every stage of an important initiative.

In the case of a major project, different bodies are often set up. Each of these must get middle managers involved or allow them representation. On a steering committee, it is essential that the main professions, departments, countries or regions affected by the initiative should be represented. You could even specifically create a committee representing 'project customers', so as to ensure that what you are constructing takes proper account of the difficulties and expectations reported by front-line management.

Within working groups developing diagnoses or solutions, it is possible to involve middle managers who act as 'opinion leaders': their participation adds credibility to the action plans that are being produced.

Lastly, from the outset, it is important to establish a community of project 'ambassadors': within each business unit, an individual is thereby given specific responsibility for listening to and informing middle managers. The individual acts as the middle managers' spokesperson at the steering committee, but also represents that committee vis-à-vis middle managers.

These various measures will give a considerable boost to your effectiveness.

In conclusion to this chapter...

You have got it: the first key to the energy of management is to treat your middle managers like VIPs.

Take this book and hand it to an employee applying for promotion to a middle management post within your company. Get the employee to ask you the following questions:

- Within your company, are middle managers valued by senior management?

- Is middle management generally seen as an asset or a burden?

- Is it given some of the credit for major successes?

- Do senior executives resist the temptation to blame middle management for every failure and every problem?

- Do your middle managers have specific rights and duties?

- Are they fully consulted before decisions on issues that they are qualified to deal with?

- Do they receive priority information, ahead of all other personnel?

- Do they enjoy true freedom of expression at meetings limited to middle management?

- Do they benefit from genuine solidarity among members of middle management?

- Do they clearly understand that, once a decision has been taken, they must loyally support it?

- When passing on decisions, do your middle managers go by the stars or do they possess a GPS?

- Do they possess communications kits to explain company decisions to their people and to allow dialogue and the personal involvement of each team?

- Do they possess practical tools designed to identify specific initiatives to be taken and to regularly monitor the progress made?

- Do they have the support of project leaders or ambassadors for each major priority so as to ensure that things are done well and efficiently?

- Do you maximize the extent to which your middle managers are involved in your project at different stages, so as to make fewer enemies and more allies?

- Are they represented on a steering committee?

- Do you treat your middle managers as you would customers?

- Do some of them participate in the development of solutions and action plans?

- If you work for a major organization, have you ensured that 'ambassadors' are appointed within the different company institutions so as to ensure that local managers feel strongly involved in the initiative?

If your candidate is unconvinced by your answers, you still have some work to do. Otherwise, move on to the next chapter.

10 Pinpoint the target

Why do middle managers never get their priorities right, when they know full well what really matters?

Start with the difficult tasks. The easy tasks will take care of themselves.

Dale Carnegie

Summary

We now focus on helping your managers to prioritize. We look at the common business disease of 'project-itis' – how the proliferation of initiatives leads to inertia. We provide guidelines on selecting priorities and then how to show your middle managers that inaction is not an option, as they are your priorities too. We finish by explaining how to change performance measures and incentivize the right behaviours.

'We need them. Don't you understand? We need them!' Nick exclaims. 'I don't just want them to be happy to work here. I want their eyes to light up when they talk to their friends about it. Don't you understand that?'

Nick is the boss of a leading mobile phone company in a large country. 'Things are going to get even more competitive in the future,' he adds. After eight years of double-digit growth, life is changing: a rapid but lasting slump in demand, the sudden emergence of new competitors, and the need to invest heavily in order to move into new technology. This is a routine occurrence in many business sectors, but a hard landing for a company used to one triumph after another.

The biannual company survey that measures the pulse of the company shows that support from his people is universal. With innovations, launches and recruitment, there is no shortage of opportunities for enthusiasm. But how can they maintain that collective energy when times get tough, cost cutting starts to bite and career prospects are restricted?

Nick has found the solution. He has made his executive committee work on a people vision: 'To have the best, most professionally contented people'.[1] Top management have also laid down some specific priorities, including: 'Recognizing performance and celebrating it across the business'. Now various working groups have issued proposals for action and compiled projects, including employee excellence awards to the most deserving staff members, whose work often goes unrecognized.

How can they make this project a success? How can they ensure that these initiatives have a genuine impact on company morale? Nothing to it: it is all up to the middle managers to promote these initiatives and projects effectively. So Nick doesn't hesitate. He sets up a steering committee, expands the remit of the external consultants and arranges for the appointment of about 50 'people vision ambassadors' company-wide to implement the projects. Above all, he calls a meeting of all the managers: firstly, the top 100 senior executives and then the 500 middle managers. He sets out his vision with conviction and explains the challenges and what he expects of each manager present in the room. This meets with almost universal approval and earns high praise: 'an inspiring vision'; 'an exciting presentation'; 'finally, a speech that recognizes how important our people are'.

Yet, three months later, the company survey reveals that the overwhelming majority of employees have never heard of the projects. Just 400 out of 5,000 surveyed have attended an employee excellence awards ceremony within their unit. Middle management have obstructed these initiatives, not out of ill will, but because of a lack of time and competing priorities that were deemed more important. That is why Nick is fuming in front of his board members: 'What on earth are they waiting for?'

Like Nick, at one time or another we have all felt exasperated with people who cannot seem to understand that priorities have changed. Perhaps it is also how others have sometimes felt about us. So why are intelligent people incapable of identifying priorities and implementing projects that they fully support?

Experience shows that middle managers may face three problems: they may feel that they are already juggling too many priorities; deep down they may believe that senior management's real priorities are not those publicized; or they may think that these are not the issues on which their performance will be judged anyway. So top managers have three duties: to hunt down mistaken priorities, to consistently champion their own project and to change the way in which performance is evaluated.

Hunt down mistaken priorities

'It is a national priority!' A former French head of state made a speciality of proclaiming new priorities. One journalist mocked this tendency, identifying 29 such priorities during the head of state's first period of office alone – of which three were described as 'even more than a priority'. Clearly, this did not make life easy for ministers, civil servants or the various tiers of public service in deciding between initiatives when resources were limited.

In business, the problem is often even worse. There is a proliferation of projects, piled one upon another or sprouting from one another. It is essential for modern organizations to operate in project mode but, as the old axiom has it, a jack of all trades is a master of none.

For a manager at head office, launching a project is a way of being useful. It must also be admitted that it is a means of establishing yourself. You just need your initiative to gain the stamp of approval in high places and to be widely publicized and implemented throughout your organization, and it is also the best possible way of building a personal profile and a bit of a reputation in-house. Thus there is no shortage of potential new projects at the corporate level. As there is a multitude of interesting subjects, it is difficult to avoid initiatives proliferating, particularly as it is generally easier to launch two projects than to halt one.

Furthermore, a fair number of initiatives come from head office and can only be implemented by middle management. So, middle managers find a plethora of corporate initiatives placed upon their shoulders, all of which are presented as priorities by their originators. They may, for example, be concerned with new management tools, customer relationship processes, marketing segmentation procedures, cost-cutting measures, outline administrative processes, quality assurance certificates, service or product launches or even new management methods, accounting standards, pricing policies or reporting rules. Good luck juggling that lot!

When there are more than three declared priorities, it generally means that in reality there are none. When there are 15, 30 or 50 projects to implement, middle managers will be unable to take everything in, to explain it and to arrange for its implementation, so they will often select their own priorities based on their own criteria. As these criteria vary from one person to another, no project (even those that are absolutely crucial to the organization) will really be implemented satisfactorily company-wide. Furthermore, the problem will usually be exacerbated from year to year, as the number of new projects deemed to be of strategic importance far exceeds the number brought to a successful conclusion.

Each champion of a head office 'priority' has the feeling that little is being done to implement their initiatives on the ground: middle management are conspiring against them. As for senior executives, like Nick they are furious to see their most crucial priorities apparently being swamped by a plethora of everyday concerns. Among the reproaches habitually made against middle management, which have you never heard – or uttered? 'Too blinkered an outlook, limited strictly to their own work and not seeing the broader picture.' 'They are more concerned with shunting complaints from staff (or customers) up the line to top management than with getting their staff (or customers) to accept the priorities stated by top management.' 'Just a conveyor belt, passing on directives without trying to give them any meaning.'

It is well known that the failure of a strategy or project is generally attributed to its poor execution: the foresight and relevance of the 'brains' behind it are rarely called into question. The fault is laid at the door of the 'foot soldiers'. What a shame it is, then, that those 'brains' do not deploy their genius to design measures that those 'foot soldiers' can convert into action, despite the fact that there are three simple principles that can be applied.

Firstly, you cannot really have more than three priorities (even three is a lot) among measures that need to be implemented widely within a company. Naturally, those measures can be broken down into various sub-projects and indicators, but those must be allocated to a small number of people with clearly identified responsibilities.[2] Indeed, if all those sub-projects descend like fine rain within an organization, it becomes impossible for middle management to identify the true priorities.

Secondly, you must avoid having different operational departments impose a flood of additional initiatives on middle management, as this will create confusion. Just as a marketing department must ensure that a particular customer is not harassed simultaneously by a series of calls, visits and mailshots from its sales force, the senior management of a company must ensure that middle managers have a very limited number of projects to implement – aside from the everyday concerns that require most of their energy.

Lastly, you cannot launch a new major project without completing at least one other.

You have to talk the talk and walk the walk

Intrigued, convinced and enthusiastic, the senior executives who listened to Nick's speech on 'people vision' supported the ideas presented to them. They heard, understood and accepted their CEO's message. Essentially, what they had to do was quite clear: they just needed to tailor the initiatives launched by the steering group to the area for which they were responsible. Those initiatives were relevant to them: furthermore, their entities were represented within the groups that had produced the action plans. Unfortunately, they did not see the promotion of this people vision as a priority. How could that be?

Many of them had taken part in 'top 100' or 'top 500' meetings for years. The main subject ('obsession', according to some) was usually market share. Nick was adamant that he reserved a ferocious hatred for their two main competitors in the mobile phone market. Each half-point of market share lost wounded him deeply and reduced him to furious rage. Each half-point gained was savoured, applauded, celebrated and generated an exciting, festive atmosphere. 'Depending on our monthly market share, you can tell in advance what the atmosphere is going to be like at the meeting,' people would often say. Market share was published in numerical format, as historical graphs, pie charts and a range of often three-dimensional geometric shapes. Causes of changes in market share were dissected, debated and sometimes argued over. Consequences were always drawn: the announcement of a new commercial partnership, the intensification of a marketing campaign, the fast-tracking of a tender launch, the adjustment of pricing policy… They moved from analysis to action in just a few hours and everyone knew why they had come and what to do next.

Aside from this, the agenda for these meetings would vary depending upon events. Obviously, profitability was a topic frequently addressed in detail. Gross margin, EBITDA, free cash flow and operating margin were chewed over, along with other ways of defining profit margins. Finance and management control specialists would comment on them. Profitability ratios per employee, per customer and per unit of turnover were compared to those of local competitors and comparable companies operating in similar countries. The mobile phone business is highly profitable, isn't it? Yes, but no shareholder is ever satisfied with that, and Nick knows it: to him it is not enough to do well; he needs to do better than everyone else – every quarter. He addresses these issues quite openly: 'My friends, we are paid to produce cash – not products or services, but cash. If one of you comes to see me in my office with a bright idea, I advise you to have three good arguments: cash, cash and more cash!'

Technical subjects also often feature. The company operates in a fast-changing business requiring massive investment. A good half of those in attendance are engineers, and there is no shortage of questions from the floor: 'Which is the best of the three options tested in the lab?' 'What lessons can we draw from the field experiments carried out on part of our infrastructure?' 'How much investment is planned for the technical upgrade to our network?' Nick is at ease with these subjects and often expresses strong convictions: 'This technological option is the one that will allow us to gain a decisive advantage over our competitors, not only for three or six months but for many years. I want you to understand that option, to adopt it and to love it.'

Lastly, other issues crop up on the agenda periodically. Customer satisfaction is one. Major efforts have been made to respond adequately to millions of subscribing customers. For example, the quality of service provided by each team, within each call centre and within each division is measured on a weekly basis. The criteria for assessment are very narrow. 'Not for one minute should you forget that we are all working for the Customer,' Nick likes to remind them. 'If the customer is not happy with our service, nothing we do serves any purpose. So think Customer, dream Customer, act Customer.'

So, what about the 'people vision'? That is something new. Furthermore, hardly anyone can ever remember staff issues having been addressed to this extent, beyond a summary of the latest results of the company survey or information about the current pay policy. The fact that it is something new makes it exciting. No doubt more ears than usual pricked up when Nick spoke. Unfortunately, that has not helped in the slightest to convince anyone that this really is a priority.

What is more, many of those who attended the meetings have already received a visit from Nick and his team. When the CEO comes to visit a regional office, events progress with military planning: a brisk tour of the premises, a few handshakes and pleasantries exchanged with staff, a short motivational speech to local middle management and, above all, an intense debate at a small committee of leading local managers. They had better be well prepared, as the questions come thick and fast: 'Give me three reasons to believe that you are going to help us to gain 1 per cent in market share within six months.' 'Are your costs competitive with those of the European market leaders? If so, prove it to me.' 'What are your three most crucial technical options? How can you prove that you are right?' 'How do you help to improve customer satisfaction? Give me two clear examples.' And so on.

So what about the 'people vision'? No, there have not been any questions about that yet. Furthermore, over the weeks following the project presentation, Nick has made five front-line visits. The issue of 'the best and most professionally contented' staff has never been put on the agenda. Ultimately, the middle managers have not yet been convinced that the 'people vision' needs to be a priority for them, because they are not really convinced that it is a priority for their CEO. Nick was clear and convincing when he spoke, yet people do not necessarily believe what they are told: they mainly look at what is done.

A priority is a red-hot issue, omnipresent, unavoidable. It is the subject that CEOs address every time that they take the stand, the issue that they ask people about when they meet them in the lift. A priority is also an issue that must become ingrained in people's minds for a certain period. Other than in the case of a sudden crisis generated by a particular event, it is rare for an issue to suddenly become a priority in most people's minds.

Having analysed the situation, Nick opts to start structuring every top 100 or top 500 managers' meeting around two issues: the 'economic vision' (including issues of market share, profitability, technology and customer satisfaction) and – systematically – the 'people vision'. For three years, not a meeting goes by without the issue being addressed, with examples, personal testimony, statistics and action plans for implementation.

That is also why whenever Nick makes a front-line visit it features presentations from local teams on achievements made in relation to the 'people vision'. Once again, they had better be prepared, as

Nick's questions come thick and fast: 'Prove to me that you have understood that the people vision is crucial to us; show me three ambitious initiatives that you have launched'; 'Are you capable of having a positive impact on your people? Present me with three key indicators'; and so on. All the middle managers quickly understand that the people vision is a genuine priority for their CEO, so it becomes a priority for them.

In short, it is by becoming a tireless, even obsessive, champion of a project that a senior manager can convince their middle management of the importance of the issue. The next stage is to show middle managers that it is their priority, too.

Put a new deal in their hands

When Lou Gerstner took up the reins at IBM in 1993, the American IT giant was on the brink.[3] A hundred thousand redundancies had not been enough to re-establish 'Big Blue's' profitability or market confidence. The only scenario envisaged by observers was for the group to be broken down into independent institutions, already nicknamed 'Baby Blues'. For his part, Lou Gerstner was absolutely convinced that there was room in the market for a very large integrator of IT solutions. IBM could survive, but to do so it would need to change its company culture.

Indeed, at that time, 'Big Blue' comprised of highly skilled teams that cooperated very little. So, when Lou Gerstner went to meet customers, he would often hear the same comments: 'It is great for you that you are the best in the world in such and such a technical field, but what would be great for me would be if you offered integrated solutions meeting my specific needs. But, to achieve that, your teams would need to start working together.' Likewise, the IBM teams loved to carry out really cutting-edge analysis and to refine the development of their products and services until they had achieved the ultimate degree of sophistication. Yet customers mainly wanted rapid access to simple solutions that worked well.

So Lou Gerstner began to send messages focusing upon customer orientation, cooperation and speed of performance to all his people. Yet he quickly realized that, despite having the theoretical support of his middle management, habits were not changing. He then learned a crucial lesson: 'People don't do what you expect but what you inspect.'[4]

More specifically, he decided to change the criteria by which everyone was now going to be 'evaluated, paid, promoted or even fired'. Those criteria incorporated teamwork and speed of execution. The performance-related bonuses paid to managers would now be linked to the profits of the corporation as a whole and no longer to those of the unit that employed them. The rest is history: a profound and rapid transformation, a spectacular economic recovery (with the creation of 40 billion dollars of market value in just four years) and a CEO who became a legend in leadership.[5]

Was it simple common sense? Maybe, yet in the overwhelming majority of companies there is a clear contradiction between what is asked of middle managers in speeches ('Make customers the priority'; 'Make our people grow'; 'Prepare for the future') and the criteria on which those same managers know that they will really be evaluated: generally, purely short-term financial indicators.

This was also one of the problems that Nick encountered from the outset with his 'people vision' project. Middle managers knew that the variable part of their pay incorporated various financial and technical parameters, but nothing connected to their CEO's declared priority, so it is not surprising that this issue did not immediately jump to the top of their list of priorities.

Therefore people vision was given a role in performance-related pay. Nick announced that the scores achieved by each unit in the company survey would now be taken into account. More specifically, two questions were selected: 'Do you feel that you have strengthened your professional skills over the last 12 months?' and 'Are you professionally happy in this company?' The positive response rate that staff in each unit gave to these two questions would determine a proportion of the bonus paid to members of middle management. In practice, this criterion only had a very marginal effect on individual pay. However, it had a major effect symbolically: everyone now understood that the 'people vision' was part of what was expected of a manager. It became a true priority.

Thus, each year, although the mobile phone market gets tougher and tougher, Nick's company survey reveals spectacular progress. Just three years after the launch of the 'people vision', the number of staff members declaring themselves to be 'professionally happy in this company' has increased by 46 per cent. The company has retained its market share despite the arrival of various new competitors, it has maintained its profitability despite falling prices, it has successfully launched 3G mobile telecoms services and it has made all its processes subject to quality assurance. Nick's gamble has paid off.

Whether you are a senior executive, middle manager, project leader or member of an executive team, announcing that something is a priority is not enough to ensure that this is really taken on board by the people responsible for implementing it on the ground. You need to hunt down mistaken priorities, to continuously champion your priority and to change the way in which performance is evaluated.

In conclusion to this chapter...

You have got it: having treated your middle managers like VIPs, the second key to the energy of management is to pinpoint the target.

Take this book and hand it to one of your middle managers. Get the manager to ask you the following questions:

- Is your new project really a priority?

- It seems to me that our company already has a lot of priorities. Which three are the most important to you?

- What plans have you made in order to ensure that head office departments do not add further priorities to these priorities?

- Quite a few other projects are ongoing and I cannot do everything. I'm well aware of the projects that you are launching, but which ones are you halting so as to ensure that there is no increase in the number of priorities?

- But is this new project really a personal priority for you? Show me you mean it: let's see if you're walking the walk.

- How much room is allowed for this subject at your various meetings, particularly ones that you organize with people directly answerable to you?

- When you visit your people on the ground, do you make it a priority to ask them questions about this subject?

- Is this new project also a personal priority for me? Have you put a new deal in my hands?

- When my work is evaluated, how will this subject be taken into account, compared to the other everyday issues for which I am accountable?

- Exactly how is this issue going to affect my fixed and variable pay?

- Could my contribution in this field have a positive or negative effect on my career development?

If your middle manager is unconvinced by your answers, you still have some work to do. Otherwise, move on to the next chapter.

Notes

1. Read *L'entreprise réconciliée* by Jean-Marie Descarpentries and Philippe Korda (Albin Michel, Paris, 2007), particularly Chapter 4.
2. Read the works on balanced scorecards, particularly Robert Kaplan and David Norton, *Alignment: Using the balanced scorecard to create corporate synergies* (Harvard Business School Press, Boston, MA, 2006).
3. Read Lou Gerstner, *Who Says Elephants Can't Dance?* (Harper Business, New York, 2004).
4. A celebrated quote by Lou Gerstner.
5. In 2008, Lou Gerstner received the Legend in Leadership Award from the prestigious Yale School of Management.

11 Compare progress

Why your people think you're asking too much of them when you should be asking for even more

That some achieve great success is proof to all that others can achieve it as well.

Abraham Lincoln

Summary

We now turn our attention to how we can motivate improvement through the effective measurement of progress. We investigate the common error of setting standardized performance targets and the problems that can result. We conclude by looking at establishing benchmarks both internally and externally to inspire enhanced performance.

Jenny is head of a network of 40 sales offices distributing IT products for business. For the past three years, their volume of customer debt has been on a continuous upward trajectory: the average customer payment time has now risen from 59 to 67 days, whereas the average in the industry is 48 days. This means that Jenny is regularly having to borrow the equivalent of more than two months' turnover (not allowing for VAT). She is at the mercy of the banks. Not only that, but they also have to bear the financial cost, at a time when future interest rates are unpredictable. Lastly, there is a high risk of losses if certain customers go bankrupt.

Jenny wants to take action: 'We've got to bring in the cash.' The five regional directors sitting around her are equally convinced that they need to become much better at negotiating with customers and at chasing them up more quickly if they are late with payments. For the past four months, the 40 branch managers and their teams have been made quite aware of this; they have been informed, trained and encouraged to take action as part of an operation named 'Cash Is King'.

They are in the midst of preparing their annual budgets, and it is clear that 'Cash Is King' will be a success only if everyone takes responsibility for meeting clear personal targets. That is where their problems begin. Jenny proposes setting a single target, applicable to all branches: to reduce payment times to 60 days, instead of 67, the current average. Yet she arouses quite contrasting reactions among her branch managers.

Jeremy, whose customer credit stands at 56 days, thinks it is a good target. For ages he has been saying that he does not understand how people can allow no-hopers to drag down the company's performance. He even willingly offers to give advice and to share his experience. Of course, he does not really see how this 'Cash Is King' initiative concerns him, as he is already far exceeding the performance level demanded. Yet Harry, whose score currently stands at 83 days, disagrees completely. 'Come to my branch and try my job.' He points out that he inherited a branch in a difficult region, with aggressive local competition, customers who are highly sensitive to payment terms, negligent administrators who had undermined the image of the branch, a team that had developed bad habits, poor customer records, etc.

Harry is quite blunt: 'Asking me to achieve 60 days within a year is completely unrealistic.'

Sales reps respond in the same way: those who are achieving good results see little motivation in this new target, while those achieving poor results cite all sorts of reasons to avoid it: their special circumstances, their distinctive customer base, their difficult area, commitments made by their predecessors, etc.

Jenny is even more astonished when she gets similar reactions from her five regional directors. Catherine, whose region is already achieving 60 days, does not really see it as an issue affecting her, whereas Patrick, whose branches are averaging 71 days, fights like the very devil to dispute the target.

Jenny realizes that the 'Cash Is King' initiative is heading for disaster. She decides to speak to each of her regional directors to institute a series of individual targets, with all regional directors then required to do likewise with their various branch managers, who in turn will be responsible for allocating targets to their sales reps. However, things get tricky once more. Jenny is amazed at the talent that each regional manager displays in trying to convince her that customer credit in the respective region is affected by three identical phenomena.

Firstly, last year's results were particularly good owing to special circumstances: in no way can they constitute a starting point when calculating the target for the year to come. Secondly, the forthcoming year looks particularly difficult, for both external and internal reasons. Thirdly, other regions are better placed to cope with more demanding targets. Taken in isolation, many of the arguments presented are beyond dispute. Jenny expends a great deal of energy trying to disprove them, one by one. Naturally, everyone has difficulties to overcome, but progress needs to be made across the board to bring in more cash; on this everyone is agreed in principle.

Jenny ends up imposing a specific target on each regional director, at the cost of some tension with several of them and, ultimately, a sense of injustice in some. Yet this is just the start of her problems. The same interminable discussions, the same tensions and the same feelings of injustice are provoked among branch managers and then among sales reps. After eight weeks of endless debate, the budget and targets are finalized. Yet the entire sales force has lost all motivation. No one believes in this project. The issue has become a source of conflict. Jenny does not know how to address the matter at meetings without provoking controversy. Meanwhile, the average customer payment time has increased from 67 to 69 days.

After reading the latest reports, Jenny sits in her office, raises her eyes to the ceiling and murmurs: 'What on earth are they waiting for?'

Why do your managers feel that you are asking too much of them?

Jenny's anxiety is very common. Setting results-based targets is often a delicate operation, requiring a combination of audacity, persuasion and, above all, plenty of determination. So why do intelligent people fight tooth and nail when targets are set, even though everyone can see that they are needed? Maybe it is because those targets are seen as unfair or unattainable or because they are based upon inappropriate data. Performance measurement is the worst system known to man, except for all the others.

Arthur Andersen, Enron, General Motors, AIG and Lehman Brothers certainly did not lack key business indicators over the months and years before they fell off the cliff. We could debate how their management control teams endlessly added new indicators, refined their measurement systems and increased the frequency with which their statistical data were circulated within different tiers of management. We can be sure that their top executives had spent hundreds of hours analysing ratios and growth percentages, during interminable meetings attended by people boasting a whole array of qualifications as well as outstanding IQs.

Yet access to a mass of data is never a guarantee that a strategy will prove successful. Numerical measurements can even have perverse effects. Indeed, the more you measure, the more you neglect what you cannot measure: such as a lack of rigour, a lack of ethics, a lack of foresight or an excess of trust.

Arthur Andersen was a victim of the leniency that some staff showed to a single client. Enron was killed off by the ethical failings of its top executives. General Motors was gradually dragged down by a failure to anticipate future trends in consumer demand. Lehman Brothers and the others paid the price for placing too much trust in complex financial products that subsequently proved 'toxic' because of bad debts.

Other companies that are in only slightly better health have been victims of another common affliction: the time taken to develop, implement and discuss statistical measurements ends up exceeding that devoted to doing the real work: taking care of people, products and customers.

Furthermore, measurement per se is of limited use unless it is converted into statistical targets for each team or individual. Thus, if a team is allocated only a small number of targets, the risk is that it will focus on just a few performance indicators – such as sales volumes – while neglecting certain key factors in success, such as customer satisfaction. Yet if too many targets are allocated, people will often quickly judge that they cannot all be achieved, so each individual will use their own discretion: 'Right, I am going to try to make a success of customer satisfaction; too bad about sales, but they were doomed this year, anyway.' The organization then loses any real control over the implementation of its strategy.

It would be easy to despair of all measurement. Yet what is not measured rarely progresses. So if a strategic initiative does not come with some indicators attached, you might as well reserve a plot in the graveyard for projects abandoned because of a lack of results.

Experience even proves that measurements must be short term in nature. The old cliché that the effects of an initiative will only be apparent in the long term should be treated with the greatest possible scepticism.[1]

So the essential question is: how can you use measurement systems intelligently and effectively?

Standardizing performance levels: another red herring

Superficially, Jenny's idea of getting all her branches to work towards a 60-day performance target is excellent. The target is clear, relevant, ambitious and realistic; it has been clearly formulated and it will be easy for everyone to compare their performance with the general target. Jenny has applied to the letter the lessons that she learned 30 years earlier at a top business school.

Indeed, within any set of entities of any nature, be they continents, countries, business units, factories, commercial branches, customers or staff, you find major differences in performance levels. This will be true whatever indicator is involved: customer credit, profitability, quality, customer satisfaction, etc. In general, there will be a certain number of high-performing entities, meaning that you will struggle to see how the others can match this. A proportion of the sample will be achieving about the average, while a significant number of institutions will be underperforming, sometimes massively so, thereby dragging down the overall result.

When a company decides to get all its teams to focus on improving a particular indicator, the commonly held idea is that they should try to achieve a consistent level of performance. As a consequence this means that priority is given to targeting improvements in those departments that are performing least well. In actual fact, this is one of the most serious errors that you could make in implementing your strategy.

Indeed, disparities in performance almost always have deep-rooted causes. The top performers possess structural assets that the others do not. These may relate to environment, infrastructure, methods, skills, 'culture' or other factors. In contrast, underperformers almost always have structural handicaps that are difficult to overcome immediately.

The first logical consequence of this is that those units that are struggling are precisely the ones that find it the hardest to achieve substantial progress. They are the ones where improvements will require the most time and energy and where change will take the longest. Of course, that is not a reason to do nothing. On the contrary, you must start to take action immediately. However, relying on these units to make significant progress for the organization as a whole is asking for bitter disappointment, yet this approach is adopted by most top executives and project managers.

The second logical consequence is that amazing sources of progress are to be found in entities that are already among the top performers. All you need to do is to ensure that the managers concerned are encouraged to improve their own performance levels, rather than to pass judgement on colleagues managing more difficult units. The major performance improvements that an organization achieves will come first and foremost from its best units.

The third consequence is that by setting a standard performance target you will simultaneously succeed in discouraging the strugglers and inducing apathy in the rest. It is hard to imagine how you could do any worse.

Thus seeking to achieve a consistent performance is not the way to achieve the best results.

Assigning individual targets: often a truly bad idea

When Jenny decides to set a specific target for each of her regional directors, she believes that she has solved the problem. Indeed, it is useful for all the directors to have a specific goal to achieve, depending upon their situation, their attributes and their limitations. This allows each director to define subsidiary targets and specific action plans and then to monitor the progress made.

In addition, assigning consistent but complementary targets to different units within an organization allows you to plan for harmonious development: the sum total of everyone's efforts will thereby mean progress is achieved.

The problem lies in getting each echelon of the organization to set a target for the tier below it. The target may be too low and may not give people sufficient impetus to change their habits, to innovate, to accelerate and to see the wider picture. Alternatively, it may be too high and may potentially stigmatize those who have accepted it as failures. Another possibility is that it is an average, thereby combining all these disadvantages. It may be that the environment (market, organization, climate, etc) proves more buoyant than anticipated and the target becomes too easy to achieve. Rewards may rain down on people who do not deserve them, as with stock option gains for mediocre senior managers when the stock market is rising. Alternatively, the environment may prove unfavourable and the target may become unrealistic and damage morale. These days, who can base targets on truly credible assumptions? Who can predict the economic growth rate, even over the coming months? Who can forecast exchange rate trends a few weeks ahead or the variations in the price of a barrel of oil over the next few days? A further possibility, and one now occurring ever more frequently, is that there might be a radical change in the environment (eg because of general restructuring or a change in strategic priorities) and a target set at the start of the year may sometimes lose all significance.

Ultimately, setting specific targets for each manager causes a lot of counterproductive behaviour. Energy devoted to 'negotiating' for the lowest possible target and to avoiding outstanding performances in excess of the target set ('We must soft-pedal and think of next year's target'), disputes over the interpretation of results, jealousy towards colleagues seen to have been given preferential treatment: none of these is designed to ease the achievement of the company's main priorities.

When, as part of a strategic initiative, you need to allocate specific targets at every level of an organization, these are additional to all the 'business as usual' indicators. There is a great risk that discussions will end up focusing on the fairness or unfairness of target allocation, instead of addressing the best way of achieving the desired outcomes.

So, if you cannot either set a performance standard or allocate individual targets, is there a way of encouraging teams to perform to the best of their abilities?

Stop ticking boxes: compare progress

When Jenny expressed her desire to achieve a performance standard of 60 days across her 40 branches and then assigned specific targets to each regional director, she essentially committed the same error: she thought that she knew the potential of the market and of her people.

Without realizing it, Jenny based her approach on the following assumptions: the market will be globally stable, our main competitors will not change their sales and marketing policies and each of my branches has a limited potential for progress. She ignored another set of assumptions. According to these, it is impossible to anticipate market trends. Customer credit may be profoundly affected, for better or worse, by changes in the behaviour of customers or competitors. Branches possess great potential for progress. Naturally, some have much greater potential than others, but it is impossible to know which.

On this basis, Jenny could have implemented her 'Cash Is King' project much more effectively. She would merely have needed to adopt these two rules: firstly, to ask each regional directorate and each branch to maximize progress in relation to the previous year, without setting any target; secondly and above all, to announce that branches would be classified by comparative progress, in relation to the number of days of customer credit allowed.

There are two ways of comparing progress.

The first method is to choose two or three relevant competitors (from among the best, not the worst) and to compare your progress to theirs, across an identical geographical area. It is true that the information may not always be instantly accessible, but it is much easier to obtain than you might think. Certain data, concerning turnover, profitability and productivity, are available from company accounts. Other more specific information is often shared within professional associations or, on a more restricted basis, between competitors who perceive a benefit in jointly ensuring greater transparency in relation to trends in their sector.

For example, 20 years ago, Jean-Marie Descarpentries, the chairman and managing director of Carnaud MetalBox, adopted a revolutionary management practice: he abandoned any reference to the company budget. All sector managers were evaluated solely in relation to improvements in performance compared to their three toughest European competitors.[2]

This comparison with the competition allows you to neutralize the effects of variations in the economic climate: if market growth slows (or accelerates), this applies to everyone. In addition, instead of producing the most cautious possible budgets and action plans (to be sure not to miss the target set), managers feel liberated to become more ambitious: they will be judged only by their capacity to do at least as well as their competitors.

In the absence of external benchmarking, the second method involves comparing different in-house units with one another. However, this comparison must definitely not relate to their performance levels in absolute terms. Progress is all that counts.

For example, one of the co-authors of this book applied this method when he was in charge of one particular business sector of a large consultancy and training company in the early years of the new millennium. The sector comprised 25 operations departments, in turn grouped into five divisions. As always, the directors of the operations departments were evaluated according to targets set following extensive negotiations over budgets. Bonuses were paid according to whether or not those targets were met. Naturally, when the climate was favourable, all or almost all managers were rewarded, even if objectively they had performed quite poorly compared to the rest of the organization. Conversely, when times were hard, all or almost all were penalized, regardless of performance. With the aim of speeding up the implementation of a strategic development project, the rules of the game were changed radically: the directors of operations departments would now be assessed on the basis of their comparative progress, using a limited number of economic and human indicators. Only those who achieved the most progress, compared to the previous year, would be rewarded. Within six months of implementation, spectacular results were achieved.

In the case of this second method, it is important to publish the classification of different units on a monthly basis, by decreasing degree of progress compared to the previous year.

Push the best to become even better

In practice, comparing progress reveals the following phenomena. Firstly, every individual, every team, indeed everyone, wants to make progress. This 'natural' aspiration is greatly stimulated by comparison with the progress of other internal or external entities. You can always dispute a target, but not the need to make progress. Secondly, those institutions whose performances are the weakest in absolute terms and whose failings are often pointed out will rediscover their pride. At last they have a feeling that they are competing on equal terms with those presented to them as role models.

In addition, those entities that are already the top performers at the outset are almost always those that make the fastest progress. Comparing progress and not performance in absolute terms gives those teams a reason once more to mobilize all their resources in order to do even better. The best become even better.

Lastly, in no way is the essential cooperation between different units hindered by comparisons of progress, even when this is done in-house. Unlike the comparison of performance in absolute terms, which often generates tension and unhealthy competition within a company, the comparison of progress promotes cooperation. When one unit is clearly progressing much faster than the average, it is proud to share the best practices that have allowed it to achieve this. The other teams, which are starting from different performance levels, have every possible motivation to pay heed to the lessons to be drawn from their colleagues' experiences.

COMPARE PROGRESS SYSTEMATICALLY

In conclusion to this chapter...

You have got it: having treated your middle managers like VIPs and pinpointed the target, the third key to the energy of management is to compare progress.

Take this book and hand it to one of your top-performing people. Get this person to ask you the following questions:

- Have you committed the error of setting a performance standard applicable to all your people? If so:

  - Is this standard an incentive to me, as one of the top performers?

  - Does it really seem achievable to those of us who are currently performing to a more modest standard?

- Have you allocated a specific target to each of us? If so:

  - Has each of your people fully accepted their target?

  - Does each of your people really view their target as an incentive?

- Have you announced that, instead of 'ticking boxes', you are now actually going to compare progress? If so:

  - Have you set simple, comprehensible measurement criteria?

  - Have you designated other companies with which a comparison is possible and appropriate?

- Have you begun to compare progress between similar units within your company? If so, have you fully explained that you are going to publish monthly progress comparisons?

If your staff member is unconvinced by your answers, you still have some work to do. Otherwise, move on to the next chapter.

Notes

1. Read or reread the old but excellent article 'Successful change programs begin with results' by Robert H Schaffer and Harvey A Thomson, in the *Harvard Business Review*, January 1992.
2. For further details of this comparative progress initiative and of events at Carnaud MetalBox, read *L'entreprise réconciliée* by Jean-Marie Descarpentries and Philippe Korda (Albin Michel, Paris, 2007), Chapter 5.

12 Make execution your trademark

Why don't your managers do what they promise, when the will is there?

Actions speak louder than words.

Proverb

Summary

We finish by focusing on how your actions can make or break the success of your strategy. We'll look at the disciplines you need to master to achieve results from your people, including prioritization, recruitment and time management. We end on an optimistic note, showing you how to radiate positivity, encourage your people to overcome obstacles and build upon success.

The atmosphere around the meeting table is gloomy. Christine, the senior manager, has arrived 25 minutes late. Meanwhile, her people have been discussing the problems they have encountered with ongoing projects; results have been disappointing and interim deadlines have been postponed time and time again. Once everyone is present, discussions turn to the key initiative for the year ahead.

Again the comments are less than enthusiastic. Bernie lets out a sigh: 'Of course, it's a good idea. Of course, we'd all like to see it come off. That would be great. But the last time we tried to carry out something similar, it didn't work, to say the least. So, here we go, heading for disaster again. As they are asking us to do it, I suppose we'll just have to get on with it, but personally I wouldn't be surprised if we run into major problems.' Frances adds: 'Same here. Overall, I'm in favour of this project. Our competitors have done it and we'll need to do it too, sooner or later. It would be a great leap forward, even a source of pride for us all. However, we must remember where we're starting from. We'll need years to get up to speed, and I'm still not sure that we really have the resources to match our ambitions.' Christine, the team manager, does her best to encourage them: 'Hey, come on! Look on the bright side. Don't be such pessimists. Let's just give it our best shot. We have targets, so let's do our best to achieve them. I'm counting on you, OK?' After an hour of discussion, Christine announces that she is expected at another meeting. Bernie and Frances shake their heads wearily. All the participants slowly close their files.

Christine watches her people as they stand up to leave. Lost in thought, she remains seated for a moment. She knows that they will all do what they can – and if there are any delays or failures to implement the action plan, those responsible will come up with convincing excuses and justifications. But why does everything take so long in this company? A worried frown crosses her face. What on earth are they waiting for? Why don't they do what they have promised?

In reality, Christine should be even more worried than she is, as she is faced with the worst possible situation. Even if she were to apply to the letter all the recommendations made in the previous chapters, she would still have to overcome a major obstacle: her organization has sunk into a culture of non-execution – and she herself is making a massive contribution to the culture without realizing it.

To eliminate such situations, there are five things that you can do: appoint middle managers who can actually take action; make doing nothing impossible; embody execution; ensure that you are personally well organized; and radiate optimism. This requires you to make execution itself a priority – and not just a priority but the highest priority of all.

Make execution your primary focus

Failure to perform is the new corporate disease. Companies do not generally lack good ideas, projects, meetings, action plans, documents, PowerPoint slides or key performance indicators. Their strategies are rarely completely misguided. On the front line, most operational decisions are taken by intelligent, experienced people who employ common sense. The almost universal problem is to ensure that you do what you promised and do it quickly and effectively at every level.

Whatever efforts are made as part of a strategic initiative to apply all the contents of the previous chapters of this book, none of it will be any good unless the company has developed a powerful execution culture. The symptoms of the disease are easy to detect. Projects drag on, schedules are continually revised and deadlines are postponed for the completion of key stages. Files accumulate, meetings proliferate and agendas are packed tight. The same subjects are discussed time and again, without any identifiable progress of note. Each year it is more difficult to allocate targets for managers, as there seem to be so many priorities. E-mail inboxes are continually full, partly because many messages are distributed en masse and copied indiscriminately to the various managers. Each team has the perfect excuse not to take the blame for blunders and poor performance.

The lack of an execution culture is a very serious problem, with many deep-seated consequences that can prove fatal to an organization. Like certain diseases, which sap an individual's willpower or immune system, the lack of an execution culture removes most of a company's capacity to act, to repel internal and external dangers and to move forward. Effectiveness is gravely affected. Initiatives already launched yield few results, and this condemns many of them to failure. Future projects are also endangered by the general scepticism that accompanies any new announcement.

Thus, these days, developing and reinforcing an execution culture at every level of an organization is more than an essential duty of any senior executive or middle manager. It is the primary focus, a meta-priority, a priority among priorities – the one upon which the success of everything else depends.

Avoid stagnation: appoint managers who drive progress forward

The 'People Review' began two hours ago. Around the table are: Maxine, the human resources director; George, the departmental director; and Catherine, the managing director. The debate turns to two executives.

Oliver is a brilliant young man. He is a graduate from a top business school, with an MBA from a US university, and his career is progressing rapidly within the company. Endowed with great analytical skills, he has always diagnosed situations exceptionally well in every new post he has taken up. Persuasive and charismatic, and completely fluent in three languages, he knows how to win over his bosses, his people and his partners to his way of thinking. Always ready to listen, naturally charming and skilful at networking, he has built up good contacts in many different company departments, and this has expanded his knowledge of the group and helped him to incorporate many different perspectives into his arguments. Ambitious and demanding, he has often changed jobs within the company, which has allowed him to accumulate a wealth of experience, particularly close to and in contact with the main decision-making hubs.

Peter has had a much more modest academic career. Analysis is not his strong suit, and he sometimes struggles to see the big picture. When he gives a presentation, his slides lack a certain professionalism, particularly as they frequently contain spelling mistakes, which he has not bothered to correct. A likeable man, who enjoys close relationships with his colleagues but who can be quick to get angry, he operates within more limited circles than Oliver. He has less experience, as he has moved rather more slowly up the promotional ladder and has spent many years in difficult operational roles far from head office. Yet he has led some large teams in complex situations and has consistently achieved much better results than the company's local competitors.

A new departmental manager needs to be appointed to replace George, who is due to take up a new posting. Oliver and Peter are in contention for the position. Unlike other decisions, which have taken a long time, this one requires just a few minutes. Maxine, the HR director, stresses Oliver's 'potential', his wealth of experience and his excellent 'cognitive and behavioural skills'. Catherine, the managing director, adds that she knows him better than Peter and that he has made a very good impression on her. Only George, the current postholder, is a little more hesitant, though unable to explain exactly why. He doesn't put any arguments forward to justify his views.

There are no black marks against Oliver: he is smart and has never failed in anything. The problem is that neither has he proven his ability to act with determination to achieve results. Peter, however, has always come up with the goods. He has accepted positions that others were quick to avoid. He has implemented difficult decisions: restructuring plans, site closures, staff redeployment initiatives. He has set up deals and won contracts. He has never thrown in the towel. It is probable that with the right people around him (including some brilliant analysts and communicators) he would make a better departmental director than Oliver. Yet, in practice, he has no chance of being offered the job.

So how do you select your future managers?

Too often, the assessment of an individual's career potential is based upon their personal marketing attributes: qualifications, quality of written expression, verbal articulacy and even physical appearance.[1] Not only is this unfair, but it is counterproductive. In reality, the best way of assessing managers' future potential is to examine their past achievements: have they continually achieved outstanding results? Have they demonstrated courage and perseverance in the face of difficulties and overcome scepticism, inertia or even opposition from others within their working environment to meet their commitments?

IQ (intelligence quotient) was long considered to be the essential criterion when selecting the elite within companies or public authorities. Yet, a few years ago, it was discovered that, when it came to achieving sustainable results, IQ was less crucial than 'EQ' – emotional quotient.[2] These days, those different quotients probably count less than what should be called 'DGTD': the Determination to Get Things Done. Sometimes, to get things done, you have to take difficult decisions: to refuse certain requests, to halt a project to which people have contributed little, and to make choices that displease people whom you really like and upon whom you rely. You also often have to take a risk by delegating and trusting others to act. You always have to convey enthusiasm and energy, to set an example and to put in even more effort than others do.

By appointing managers who are mainly oriented towards analysis or office politics, we are responsible for discouraging their teams, thwarting our strategic initiatives and undermining the credibility of our own leadership. Don't!

Once managers are appointed for their ability to act, all that remains is to introduce – and above all abide by – operational rules that are clear and transparent to all. This will ensure that action is taken as a matter of course.

Make doing nothing impossible

The annual appraisal interview has just begun. As the manager of a head office department responsible for public relations and lobbying, Claudia has been unable to meet her targets. Her budget has had to be increased during the past year, she has been unable to carry out certain activities aimed at contributing to the new strategy and the team's work has continued to focus mainly upon the same old tasks.

Alex, the CEO, is annoyed. This is not the first time that Claudia has failed to deliver the results expected, but she does have some excuses. The general business climate has made life tricky, her team has been undermined by internal rivalries and Claudia has probably done her best. She has held this post for more than 10 years and has acquired certain habits that sometimes make it difficult to point her in the direction of new priorities. Not only that, she is extremely thin-skinned, and the slightest criticism can lead to raised voices, tears and lost working time.

So Alex listens in silence as Claudia explains all the difficulties that she has had to cope with. When the time comes for him to raise the issue of her annual bonus, he wonders, as the sums at stake are quite small to the company as a whole, whether he should run the risk of not giving Claudia the reward that she is expecting. He quietly points out to her that 'strictly speaking' she has not met her targets, but he quickly adds that, in view of her hard work and ability, Claudia does indeed deserve the size of bonus that she is expecting. At the end of the interview, he has the feeling that he has done his job. Well, he would say that, wouldn't he?

It is an essential part of the management code that you should clearly differentiate between how you treat execution and non-execution.[3] Performance must be rewarded. Bonuses and promotions must go to the 'doers' who take the initiative, put in the maximum effort, meet their commitments and deliver the results expected.

What if the results are not forthcoming? Ultimately, you have five options, with implications ranging from minor to major.

The first is to help the person to make rapid progress in their work. Listen, coach, demonstrate, demand, observe, debrief, highlight and celebrate each instance of progress. That takes time, but it is often time well spent. We often underestimate individuals' ability to act if they have the time to build up their confidence and expertise.

The second, harsher, option is to apply a penalty or, at least, to withdraw a reward. Indeed, if you do not make a clear distinction between those who deliver and those who do not, you are quickly going to discourage those who take the risk of delivering, as they will soon wonder why they bother.

The third option involves responding to inaction by assigning the person to other duties: there the person will have a second chance to demonstrate their abilities, while enabling you to offer another person the opportunity to succeed where the first person failed. In the case of a managerial position, the confidence and morale of a whole team may be boosted as a result.

The fourth, and most drastic, course of action with someone guilty of doing nothing, particularly a manager, is to show them the door. By allowing those who produce hot air and little else to go and work for the competition, you are a winner twice over. However, as John Kotter, guru of change management,[4] suggests, you must be careful to distinguish between sceptics and those who habitually drag their feet. Sceptics wait until they are completely convinced before showing commitment, but may then make a valuable contribution to progress. However, a habitual foot-dragger is a manager who uses not only inaction but also criticism and cynicism to systematically undermine reform initiatives introduced by a company. According to Kotter, such people must be ruthlessly removed from positions where they can do damage. Sceptics deserve greater consideration.

Lastly, the fifth option is to wait until your own boss (or board) adopts one of the first four options and applies it to you. This is by far the preferred attitude of the greatest number. It may be dressed up in all sorts of excuses: 'I have other priorities right now; things will sort themselves out'; 'The important thing is not to do things quickly, but to do them well'; 'You can't expect instant success'; etc.

It is up to you.

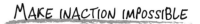

Embody execution

The meeting of the business unit management team is scheduled to last from 9 am until noon, and the main item on the agenda is to monitor progress with their strategic project. John, the senior manager, has been delayed by a conference call with China. When he enters the room at 9.20 am, his team members are busy dealing with e-mail messages. Two of them are on the phone, while a third has gone to sort out an urgent problem. After a few minutes, the meeting is able to start, with just one person missing. John starts the meeting by giving an informal report on the outcome of his conference call that morning. Their Chinese partners have raised further issues for negotiation, but the potential turnover still seems higher than initial forecasts. A discussion takes place about the attitude that they should adopt towards these partners. Two of the participants exchange rather heated views on the subject. One of them believes that they should fast-track the signing of the contract, while the other warns the group against the risks involved in 'rushing into things'. John calms them down and suggests that they return to the agenda. The first item on the agenda is an update from each participant on the progress so far on the strategic project. By then it is already 10.05 am, over an hour into the meeting, and several of the participants say that there are more pressing issues to address. Ignoring the official agenda, they agree to start with these issues.

There is an intense discussion as to whether or not a dispute with another unit about a complex in-house purchasing issue should be referred to the group board for resolution. One of the participants then points out that a 15-minute coffee break was scheduled for 10.30 am and he needs to absent himself for half an hour in order to meet a customer. In the event, the coffee break lasts for 45 minutes. The issue of the dispute with the other unit is postponed and referred back to a subcommittee. Other issues are quickly dealt with. With the scheduled end of the meeting in sight, there are just 25 minutes remaining to review the principal item on the agenda, the strategic project. John rapidly goes round the table, sounding out all those present on their views on the situation. There are a number of tricky problems, including a lack of communication between departments and imprecise operating rules. It quickly becomes apparent that little progress has been made. John decides to call another meeting focusing solely on these issues. As they all have very busy schedules, they are unable to agree a date when everyone can attend, so they decide that they will get their assistants to find a date, even if that means rearranging other meetings. This meeting must take place within three weeks, maximum. John is more than a little frustrated at this turn of events, but at least he has been able to see the scale of the obstacles yet to be overcome, so perhaps the meeting was of some use.

At least, that is what he thinks. In reality, he has just given his entire team licence not to implement the strategy. The meeting started late; the first item discussed was not even on the agenda; the attention of some participants was diverted elsewhere. The issue that should have been discussed, the strategic project, wasn't even mentioned till halfway through the meeting. The message that came through was: 'Don't worry about the strategic projects; there are other more urgent priorities.' John, the chair of the meeting, failed to set an example, allowed himself to be sidetracked and was thus in no position to demand that all other participants attend the meeting from beginning to end. By postponing consideration of the main issue to the end of the meeting and allowing opinions to be expressed off the cuff, he excused those attending from any need to report on action taken to meet commitments arising from the previous meeting. By then postponing the issue to a subsequent meeting, he allowed his team to 'freewheel' without any roadmap. Three more weeks are bound to be lost. Overall, his conduct induced apathy among his people and helped to reinforce the culture of non-performance prevalent within his team.

Every senior executive and every middle manager must embody execution.[5] Many are unaware of this. However, there are a few simple rules that should be applied under all circumstances.

The way in which meetings are organized is a prime example of this. Every manager should, without fail, begin every meeting by obtaining an update from every participant on the actions that they have taken in response to the action list of the previous meeting. No meeting should end without each participant making a commitment to carry out a specific set of actions immediately. Each participant must be absolutely clear that rigorous and frequent monitoring will take place and that excuses and justifications will not be accepted: commitments must be met.

In the context of strategy implementation, managing timescales is equally important. If you announce an initiative, start it immediately. If you receive a call or an e-mail about strategy implementation, respond within half a day unless there are exceptional circumstances. If you have to arrange a meeting on the subject, find a slot within a week.

Is that too much to ask? If you cannot be sufficiently responsive in implementing strategic decisions, it is probably because you have allowed your schedule to get clogged up with too many secondary issues. Delegate. Don't get involved in meetings on non-crucial issues. Limit your trips away. Do not allow your people to pass the buck to you.

Follow Gandhi's advice: 'You must be the change that you want to see in the world.' Set an example. Be a role model. Embody performance.

Stop relying on your memory

Stephanie is distraught. 'My people are getting nowhere; they seem to get confused by all the changes that are imposed on them. I try to explain things to them in simple terms and they seem to understand, but nothing happens. They are constantly firefighting. They just can't see the bigger picture.' As the words leave her mouth, Stephanie takes a glance around her own office. She sees heaps of files, while loose pages covered in handwritten notes are scattered around in places where they should not be. There are about 15 Post-it notes listing the phone numbers of people to call back or tasks to be completed. Then she realizes that she has half a dozen other commitments of which she has no record whatsoever. How can we criticize others when we are guilty of acting in the same way?

If you do not have a clear overview of your commitments, it is almost certain that you are letting down some of the people who rely on you. You are contributing to the culture of non-execution.

The most effective method is probably that proposed by David Allen,[6] which relies upon a few simple words of advice:

> Clear your mind of absolutely every unnecessary encumbrance: make a note of everything that you have to do on a limited series of lists (or get someone else to do so). Set up these lists by location or situation: tasks to be carried out in the office, telephone calls to make, issues to raise with particular colleagues etc. You can thereby free up your brain's RAM for essential issues. Within those lists group together everything that is recorded elsewhere: Post-it notes, notes on files, etc. Among all the information in these lists, distinguish between tasks of four types. Tasks that take less than two minutes must be carried out immediately to avoid wasting time recording them and going back to them. Others can be delegated and then followed up with the person concerned. Other actions can be put off to a later date. Finally other actions, which require the involvement of other people, should be treated as projects in their own right, using a checklist drawn up for the purpose. If you cannot do everything, you must make an informed decision as to which tasks you are not going to do. Give precedence to your priorities. Use your abilities to maximize your contribution to the practical implementation of initiatives prioritized by your company.

Never forget that the greatest of strategies often fail because of minor details. Rolling out a strategic initiative throughout an organization involves a multitude of details in the hands of a large number of people. You cannot cover for everyone. Yet, whatever your role within the organization, you can ensure that your personal contribution sets an example. That alone is of great assistance.

Radiate optimism

From the case study at the beginning of the chapter, when Christine sees her colleagues Bernie and Frances leave the meeting, she can tell that implementing her main project is going to be hard work. Her people are very well aware of the need to act and sincerely want the initiative to be successful. However, they do not 'believe in it'. Often the main obstacle to action is neither a lack of support nor a lack of ability, nor even a lack of goodwill. It is discouragement.

The world-famous psychologist Martin P Seligman[7] has been studying this phenomenon for 30 years. His research demonstrates that optimism plays an essential role in our propensity to triumph over adversity in every field, including health, sport and working life. Obviously, it is not a case of waiting passively for positive outcomes to occur of their own will, but of being convinced of your own ability to influence the course of events. Seligman's research also indicates that discouragement is a 'learned' phenomenon. When confronted with failure, individuals tend to become discouraged if they perceive the reasons for this to be general and permanent. These perceived reasons may be internal: 'I do not have the right personality for this type of work'; 'I have never really felt comfortable at handling tense situations.' They may also be external: 'Our customers are hostile to innovation'; 'Our company culture does not encourage this sort of initiative'; 'We are not strong enough to take on the major players in the sector.'

Once discouragement sets in about one specific issue, it tends to spread to all of an individual's activities. For example, an individual who is discouraged by failing a language test will tend to give up on completing a puzzle, even though the two activities do not require the same skills. Furthermore, discouragement spreads rapidly within a social group. It encourages capitulation and then failure. In turn, this reinforces a feeling of impotence and discouragement, which then goes on to affect other activities.

The good news is that optimism can be learned, too, both by individuals and within an organization – and you can contribute to this in three ways.

Firstly, you can contribute through your own behaviour. Without denying the scale of the difficulties, show that you are absolutely convinced, at all times and in all circumstances, of the ability of your teams to influence the course of events. Assurance, confidence and enthusiasm are just as contagious as doubt, anxiety and helplessness.

Secondly, you can help your people to attribute setbacks (which are avoidable if you take action) to specific reasons and to causes that can be overcome in the future: 'During the initial phase, we did not get our customers sufficiently involved in development work, but we are going to put that right'; 'You still lacked experience of such operations, but now you have learned a lot'; 'Our competitor responded with great vigour because we slipped up at the worst possible moment, but the situation is completely different now.'

Lastly, you can connect each success to an ongoing, general cause, which will yield further success in the future: 'You succeeded because you were able to make perfect use of the different skills at the department's disposal; that was crucial and will be again in the future'; 'We achieved good results immediately because our company culture suits projects of this type'; 'Our competitor was unable to respond because they are never as quick as us when we really get behind an action plan.'

By exuding optimism, you give your teams the energy that they need in order to overcome difficulties.

In short, the development of a management performance culture is one of the major challenges for any organization. Whatever your role, you can contribute to this by helping to promote people who have proven their ability to act, by setting an example and abiding by your own commitments, by monitoring the commitments of others and by showing your ability to instil active optimism.

In conclusion to this chapter...

You have got it: having treated your middle managers like VIPs, pinpointed the target and compared progress, the fourth key to the energy of management is to make execution your trademark.

Take this book and hand it to a stranger. Get the stranger to ask you the following questions:

- On the last occasion when you helped to select a middle manager, which criteria did you prioritize?

    - Intellectual qualities or the determination to act?

    - Potential or achievements?

    - Cleverness or courage?

- On the last occasion when one of your people failed to meet their commitments, how did you respond?

- Did you really accept your responsibilities?

- Are you the personal embodiment of an execution culture?

- Does each of your meetings begin with each person giving an update on commitments made at the previous meeting?

- Does each of your meetings end with each participant making specific commitments?

- Do you respond to every e-mail or phone call about an essential issue within half a day? Do you find time for any further meeting on this issue within a week?

- Are you personally sufficiently well organized to enable you to meet your commitments?

- Are all the tasks that you need to complete collected on a small number of easily accessible lists?

- Do you immediately carry out any task taking less than two minutes?

- Are you fully aware of the tasks with which you are behind schedule?

- Do you radiate optimism?

- Do you show that you are absolutely convinced, under all circumstances, of your team's ability to influence the course of events?

- Do you systematically help your people to attribute failures to specific reasons and surmountable causes?

- Do you systematically help them to connect each success to a general, ongoing cause, which will yield further success in the future?

It doesn't matter that much whether or not the stranger understands your answers. Whatever the situation, the time has come to put aside this book and get ready to take action!

Notes

1. For example, read 'Attractiveness and corporate success' by ME Heilman and MH Stopeck, in *Journal of Applied Psychology*, 1985, **70** (2), pp 379–88.
2. See *Emotional Intelligence: Why it can matter more than IQ,* by Daniel Goleman (Bantam, New York, 1995).
3. Read *Execution: The discipline of getting things done,* by Larry Bossidy and Ram Charan (Crown Business, New York, 2002).
4. Read his classic *Leading Change* (Harvard Business School Press, Boston, MA, 1996).
5. Read, *inter alia, A Sense of Urgency,* by John Kotter (Harvard Business School Press, Boston, MA, 2008).
6. David Allen (2003) *Getting Things Done: The art of stress-free productivity,* Penguin Books, New York.
7. In particular, read his marvellous book *Learned Optimism* (Free Press, New York, 2004).

Conclusion

All people organizations (associations, unions, schools, universities, governments, armies, authorities, local councils or NGOs) face the same challenges: to find the energy to implement decisions at every level, to transform ideas into action and to turn principle into practice.

Of course, initially the essential task is to identify the goals we want to achieve, the causes we wish to serve or the problems we have to resolve. Yet this is usually quite clear. Action is the priority – more specifically the action of your people.

If we extend this to issues affecting society as a whole (tackling global warming, protecting air and water quality, preventing accidents and diseases, promoting public-spiritedness and tolerance, etc), progress can often be achieved only by changing public habits. Generally, we are all well aware of what we should do – but we do not manage to do it, at least not often or quickly enough. The issues addressed in this book therefore go well beyond the limited sphere of business.

We live in a blame culture. When faced with inaction, we systematically look to point the finger, preferably at someone powerful or out of reach: 'the prime minister', 'the law', 'the Americans', 'the Chinese', 'politicians', 'vested interests', 'attitudes', etc. The main effect of this is that we do not have to question our own ability to take the initiative. However, it is you that this book is all about. Taking responsibility for what you can and should do is the key message.

This book suggests ways in which you can instil energy. This energy can encourage personal commitment by ensuring that your message is delivered, heard, understood and accepted and that it generates enthusiasm. This energy can change habits by developing company culture, skills and the promotion of best practices. It can allow you to take full advantage of management structures by using them to channel decisions effectively, focusing on real priorities, stimulated by a thirst for progress and obsessed by performance. Ultimately, however, your only true power is over yourself. The rest is a question of leadership. This concept is defined as the art of getting other people to do things that they probably would not have done of their own will (at least not as well or as quickly). We shall therefore end this book by recommending four literary works that will give you the tools to assess how you, as a leader, should direct your energy.

Covey, or the importance of initiative

The first tool is taken from Stephen R Covey's famous book *The Seven Habits of Highly Effective People*. In the book, the author demonstrates that one of the characteristics of effective leaders is the capacity to draw a clear distinction between the sphere of their concerns and their sphere of influence. The first sphere contains everything that is of concern to us: today's weather, traffic, the health of loved ones, international conflicts, etc. This sphere may be quite extensive. Its contents can endlessly fuel our thoughts, discussions and emotions. The second, much smaller, sphere is located within the first. It contains those issues over which we can exert some influence. These affect our work, our close family, the various communities to which we belong, and our (generally modest) contribution to much greater causes.

We all spend much too much time considering and discussing subjects over which we have no real influence. This drains us of energy, and also applies to someone who continually worries about a sick loved one or who regularly complains about the weather or about having to comply with an inconvenient new law.

Instead, we should focus upon where we have room for manoeuvre. We cannot cure a sick relative, but maybe we can offer useful psychological or practical support. We cannot change the weather, but maybe we can adapt our schedule or equipment. We cannot change a new law, but maybe we can use it as an opportunity to improve certain practices.

Covey demonstrates that the more we concentrate on our sphere of influence, the more we gradually succeed in expanding it. So it is absolutely essential that we take the initiative. To do this, we need to find our true position vis-à-vis the other people concerned. It is here that the writings of Eric Berne may help us.

Berne, or the choice of life position

In the 1960s, the US psychiatrist Eric Berne developed and popularized the concept of 'transactional analysis', some of whose tools are still very useful in better understanding and overcoming certain difficulties in everyday life.[1] In particular, Berne explains that we tend to adopt four distinctive 'life positions', which can largely determine the success or failure of our actions, especially our influence over others. Ask yourself which of these positions you adopt when dealing with an important issue that comes within your remit.

We are characterized as adopting the '+ −' position if we believe that problems are caused by other people. It may be that our life history or social status or even how others behave towards us will predispose us to such an attitude. Thus, when struggling to get things done, a top executive needs exceptional humility not to think: 'My decisions are correct. It is the others (the team, middle management or front-line staff) who have not yet taken the action required in order to deliver.'

This 'life position' leads us to neglect the actions that we ourselves could take, and above all it directs our energy against others. It means that we condemn our people to a position of inferiority that encourages childish behaviour. Instead of initiative, it generates passive submission. Instead of constructive proposals, it encourages criticism, sarcasm or even opposition. As part of a vicious cycle, such behaviour in turn tends to reinforce the manager's belief that their people lack intelligence, commitment or a sense of responsibility.

The '– +' position is the one that paralyses us when we do not feel that we are up to the job. For example, a young project manager with no formal hierarchical authority may feel intimidated when faced with more experienced senior executives endowed with powerful personalities. 'They don't listen to me or take me seriously.' 'It's not as if I'm going to ask to address the board. They've got much bigger fish to fry.'

This position leads us to direct our energy against ourselves, to engage in self-censorship and to keep our counsel. It prevents us from occupying ground that could be accessible to us – and from opening it up to others.

The '– –' position is the one that we adopt when we see ourselves as victims. That is what happens when we attribute malicious intent or destructive behaviour to others, while denying that we have any ability to exert an influence over the course of events: 'They're just trying to undermine my plans. They incessantly criticize the detail, but what can I do about it? It would have served no purpose, anyway.'

This position leads to discouragement and capitulation. It leaves us devoid of energy.

Particularly when you occupy a leadership role, the only effective life position is '+ +', which implies both self-confidence and esteem for others. It is the attitude adopted by a manager who says: 'They are still standing in the background, which is to be expected. They have drawn my attention to problems that I had not really taken into account. For my part, I'll be able to improve my plan and I'm sure that I'll be able to convince them.'

On paper, adopting this '+ +' life position is the obvious solution. Yet, if you look around you at managers who are struggling to get other people to take action, you will find that in most cases part of the problem resides in the 'life position' adopted by the individual leader. So, when we ask 'What on earth are they waiting for?' we must also ask whether our own mindset is tuned into the '+ +' position.

Once we are ready to take the initiative and are settled in our life position, we need to ask ourselves about the qualities that must be deployed to provide effective leadership and to encourage others to take action. Here, it is the philosopher Peter Koestenbaum who can provide us with a few clues.

Koestenbaum, or the acceptance of the challenge

The philosopher Peter Koestenbaum espouses a simple and interesting theory of leadership.[2] He says that an individual must find their place by developing four qualities consisting of two pairs of polar opposites: vision and a sense of reality, ethics and courage. Without a sense of reality, great foresight is no guarantee of a successful outcome. However, without foresight, a sense of reality is insufficient. Yet it is difficult to combine these two qualities spontaneously. When we struggle to motivate others, no doubt it is because we have underestimated one of these two dimensions. Likewise, it is easy to talk about ethics when we do not have the courage to act. Yet decisions and actions (which may be difficult or even painful) do not constitute true leadership if they lack essential respect for values and principles. Here again, we can clearly see how both a lack of ethics and a lack of courage can create many practical problems affecting performance within our organizations.

No one is perfect. No one can simultaneously be an outstanding visionary, a champion of realism, an ethical role model and the epitome of courage. It is a matter of identifying which of these dimensions (vision, reality, ethics or courage) we need to work harder at, so as to avoid weakening our capacity to energize others.

Koestenbaum invites us to confront this lack of rigour by moving beyond our anxiety:

> Anxiety leads to action. The opposite of despair is to will to be that self which one truly is. That is the experience of anxiety. Anxiety is the experience of thought becoming action. What do you feel when reflection becomes behaviour, when theory is transformed into practice? Anxiety is pure energy. Anxiety that is denied makes us ill. Anxiety that is fully confronted and fully lived through converts itself into joy, security, strength, centeredness and character. The practical formula is: Go where the pain is.

Lastly, in order to get an entire organization moving, we need to draw inspiration from Jean-Marie Descarpentries, a benchmark authority on this subject.

Descarpentries, or the inverted pyramid

As the former boss of Carnaud MetalBox and Bull, admired throughout his career for his outstanding results and anointed by the US *Fortune* magazine as one of the 'most fascinating business leaders in the world', Jean-Marie Descarpentries invented and experimented with new approaches to leadership.[3] In particular, he relied upon the inverted pyramid concept initially developed by the Swede Jan Carlzon, then boss of the SAS airline. Carlzon believed that traditional organizations tended to crush employees and neglect customers, giving undue power to senior executives and administrative departments. He recommended maximizing the autonomy of staff in direct contact with customers and then placing the rest of the organization at their service. Descarpentries picked up and enriched this concept so as to use it even more boldly: maximum delegation, the principle of trust, the elimination of budgets as a central management tool and the promotion of disorder as a factor in progress.

Above all, though, he demonstrated that the crucial factor was to develop leaders at every level of an organization. Ultimately, he confronted us with the following ideas. If, above all, you want your people to be obedient, you will probably achieve this. However, you will not encourage your teams to display initiative, creativity or a passion for customers and projects. In contrast, it is by offering an inspiring vision and by placing yourself at the service of your teams that you will instil the energy that will guarantee that your most crucial plans will be implemented.

A closing comment

It is time for you to stop reading this book and to return to the task in hand. Perhaps you feel discouraged at the scale of the task. Maybe you opened this book wondering what on earth others were waiting for and why they were not taking action. Maybe you are closing it again with the feeling that the ball is in your court. Of course, it would have been easier for you to have joined the ranks of those who choose to remain passive: those who prefer to complain rather than to act. There are many who do adopt this approach, and they are never short of arguments to attract new recruits. Unfortunately for them, but fortunately for those who are counting on you, you have moved beyond their siren call.

So, from among the ideas stimulated by this book, select two or three priorities for action – and do them now!

Notes

1. Ian Stewart (2007) *Transactional Analysis Counselling in Action*, Sage, Newbury Park, CA.
2. For example, read *Leadership: The inner side of greatness, a philosophy for leaders* (Jossey-Bass, San Francisco, CA, 2002).
3. Read *L'entreprise réconciliée*, co-written with Philippe Korda (Albin Michel, Paris, 2007), to which the DCF, the French Sales and Marketing Executives' Association, awarded its 2008 prize.

Appendix: Checklists

Part 1: *The energy of engagement*

Chapter 1: Open the box of secrets

Provide true inspiration... and explain the situation	Yes	More or less	No, not yet
Have you presented the positive reason or opportunity?			
Have you overcome your own fears (damage to troop morale, leaks of information, being in the firing line)?			
Have you placed sufficient trust in people and their ability to understand what is at stake?			
Have you taken account of the fact that, however much information people receive, they need help to interpret it constructively?			

Be direct: explain your plan	Yes	More or less	No, not yet
Have you presented your plan to all those people capable of helping to implement it?			
Have you fully appreciated how a change that may be minor to you can be important to others?			
If your plan is confidential for now, have you identified the point at which you will need to inform the people concerned?			
Have you provided your people with very clear information, as they are already drowning in a flood of data?			
Spell it out: tell them exactly what they have to do	Yes	More or less	No, not yet
Are you capable of putting into a few words exactly what you expect of each individual?			
Have you taken the time to explain this to them?			

Chapter 2: Capture everyone's attention

Talk their language and pique their curiosity	Yes	More or less	No, not yet
Did you start by talking to them about themselves?			
Did you make connections between your project and their own main concerns?			
Did you show them the extent to which they personally have a crucial role to play?			

Talk less – but differently	Yes	More or less	No, not yet
Is your message brief, clear and incisive?			
Do you adopt a distinctive, innovative tone?			

Tune in and turn on	Yes	More or less	No, not yet
Do you talk to them both about the anticipated benefits and about the risks of inaction?			
Have you clearly highlighted the goal that is to be achieved? Have you also specified the stages en route?			
Does your message refer both to people and to tools, procedures and tasks?			

Chapter 3: Spell it out in words of one syllable

Don't just give information: tell a story	Yes	More or less	No, not yet
Are the words you use clear and specific?			
Have you thought up three or four essential messages, each comprising: no more than 3 to 10 words; a specific verb; a complete lack of ambiguity?			
Do you take the trouble to tell people a story when you tell them about your project? If so, is that story: moving? funny? Does it allow each individual to fully understand and remember what you hope to achieve together?			

Spell it out: show them they must act	Yes	More or less	No, not yet
Has your general message been specially tailored to each category of people, or even to each individual concerned?			
Have your people been shown specific examples of initiatives taken by particular colleagues?			
Have you assigned short-term objectives to each individual and shown how these can be followed up?			

Chapter 4: Mould opinion

They don't believe that the problem exists	Yes	More or less	No, not yet
Do the people you work with think that it is a problem too?			
Have they understood the cause of the problem?			
Do they think that the problem is important too?			
They don't believe in the solution	Yes	More or less	No, not yet
Do the people you work with also think that it is a great solution to their important problem?			
The decision taken conflicts with some of their interests or values	Yes	More or less	No, not yet
Do they think that the plan works against their interests?			
When they go home, are they proud to talk about it?			

Come on! Put yourself in their shoes for a minute	Yes	More or less	No, not yet
Have you identified allies who will win over the 'undecideds'?			
Have you changed things so as to win more allies?			

Stop moaning and set an example	Yes	More or less	No, not yet
Are you sure that you are walking the walk as well as talking the talk?			

Sorting things out from the top down: get your middle managers onside first	Yes	More or less	No, not yet
Have you started from the top, by ensuring that you have the support of your top executives?			

Open the windows: let your message come from outside, too	Yes	More or less	No, not yet
Have you looked outside your company for people who could help you to explain things?			

Hold your head up high and appeal to values	Yes	More or less	No, not yet
Have you shown them the important things that won't change?			

Chapter 5: Provide an emotional spark

Right, they've understood! Now it's your turn	Yes	More or less	No, not yet
Have you taken the time to listen to them properly?			
Have you been able to listen to their problems without rushing to prescribe solutions?			
Have you publicly recognized how difficult the task is for the people concerned?			
Have you listed, face to face, the main obstacles that they may struggle to overcome?			
If necessary, have you employed an external specialist to carry out a fuller listening exercise?			
Appreciate they need to be appreciated: they'll appreciate it	Yes	More or less	No, not yet
Have you done enough to boost the prestige of the best performers?			
Have you demonstrated your genuine recognition of skills?			
Have you highlighted and encouraged initial efforts and early (even modest) progress?			
Have you granted individuals true personal recognition?			
Minds switched on? Now win their hearts	Yes	More or less	No, not yet
Have you created positive emotions around your project?			
Have you taken some everyday initiatives?			
Have you organized or used events in order to generate enthusiasm?			

Sparkle and be on top of your game	Yes	More or less	No, not yet
Have you demonstrated your determination?			
Have you demonstrated your confidence in your ability to succeed?			
Have you demonstrated your enthusiasm about this project?			

Part 2: The energy of change

Chapter 6: Lift them out of their comfort zone

Let's talk culture	Yes	More or less	No, not yet
In a few words, can you describe the 'culture' of your company and/or your team?			
Have you identified its positive aspects?			
Have you identified the habits that you would like to change, so as to enable you to implement your new priorities more effectively?			
Reshuffle the pack to change their hands	**Yes**	**More or less**	**No, not yet**
Are you going to 'reshuffle the pack' to make organizational changes?			
Can you quite simply change the 'route map' for people and ideas within your working areas?			

Stop using old language: change your vocabulary	Yes	More or less	No, not yet
Are you going to change certain job titles so that people develop a new image of their role?			
... or the names of particular institutions?			
... or the names of particular meetings?			

Inspire dreams and celebrate new champions	Yes	More or less	No, not yet
Have you identified the people from outside your organization whom you could present as role models?			
Have you identified people in-house who could be better used as an example to others of new behaviour to be adopted?			

Be a guru and introduce new rituals	Yes	More or less	No, not yet
Have you identified the new rituals that you could introduce on a daily, weekly, monthly or annual basis to create new habits that will help to ensure that your priorities are put into practice?			

Chapter 7: Let talent out of the closet

Where possible, make training courses obsolete	Yes	More or less	No, not yet
At every stage of your project, have you sought to limit the number of habits that the different people involved have to change?			
Have you provided your people with a knowledge base allowing them instant access to information required at their workplace or from their workstation?			
Have you ensured that your people receive assistance from a tool or an individual providing step-by-step guidance at the precise moment when they carry out a task for the first time?			

If training is required, train everyone immediately	Yes	More or less	No, not yet
Have you defined training objectives very precisely? In particular...			
... the two or three simple messages that your people must remember?			
... those few items of information that they must learn by heart?			
... the actions and behaviour required in a few specific and well-defined situations?			
Have you employed innovative teaching methods to train larger groups in less time?			
Have you ensured that part of the training time will be devoted to real work?			
Have you checked that each of your people was trained on a just-in-time basis?			

Teach less, train more	Yes	More or less	No, not yet
Is the training tailored quite specifically to the main situations that your people encounter?			
Is the bulk of the programme devoted to focused practice?			
Is that training based upon real circumstances that the participants deal with? Is it carried out on the job?			

Ignite a spark	Yes	More or less	No, not yet
Have you given meaning to the work required, by connecting it to worthwhile outcomes?			
Have you boosted your people's confidence by putting each of them in a situation where they can succeed via simple, repeated exercises?			
Have your people taken pleasure from getting trained?			
Have you used the dynamism particular to large groups?			
Have you given each of them an opportunity to put their personal strengths to specific use?			
Have you appointed enthusiastic trainers who are good at teaching?			

Plan for the future now	Yes	More or less	No, not yet
Have your middle managers been trained after top management but before your staff?			
Has specific provision been made for line managers to prepare for the training of each staff member and to then support them when they put what they have learned into practice?			
Have you equipped your line managers with the tools required to ensure that they can play their role in promoting training?			

Chapter 8: Make excellence contagious

Be a meddler and identify the habits of top performers	Yes	More or less	No, not yet
Have you really selected the best practices by watching those who are making the best progress?			
Have you sorted and then formalized those ideas so as to make them fully usable?			
Have you also identified how other top-performing companies operate in other business sectors?			

Don't be prescriptive: offer them options from a menu	Yes	More or less	No, not yet
Have you resisted the desire to impose additional rules and constraints?			
Have you given them the opportunity to consider a range of good practices so as to choose those that would be the most useful to each of them, according to their particular circumstances?			
Have you arranged for those practices to be deployed throughout the organization? Has each of your people been able to get involved?			
Adopt the toothbrush strategy: no debate, just daily application	**Yes**	**More or less**	**No, not yet**
Are your people supervised and encouraged every day for the first few weeks?			
Do you frequently and systematically measure the progress achieved?			

Part 3: The energy of management

Chapter 9: Treat your middle managers like VIPs

Middle management: one of the worst jobs in the world	Yes	More or less	No, not yet
Are they generally seen as an asset rather than a burden?			
Are they given some of the credit for major successes?			
Do senior executives resist the temptation to blame them for every failure and every problem?			

Make them feel special: build a community	Yes	More or less	No, not yet
Are they amply consulted before decisions on issues that they are qualified to deal with?			
Are they specially informed, before all other personnel?			
Do they enjoy true freedom of expression at meetings limited to middle management?			
Do they benefit from genuine middle management solidarity?			
Do they clearly understand that, once a decision has been taken, they must loyally support it?			
Go by the stars if you wish, but make sure you give your middle managers a GPS	Yes	More or less	No, not yet
Do they possess communications kits to explain company decisions to their people and to allow dialogue and the personal involvement of each team?			
Do they possess practical tools designed to identify specific initiatives and to regularly monitor the progress made?			
Do they have the support of project leaders or ambassadors for each major priority so as to ensure that things are done well and efficiently?			
Make fewer enemies and more allies	Yes	More or less	No, not yet
Are they represented on a steering committee? Are they treated as 'project customers'?			
Do some of them contribute to the development of solutions and action plans?			
If you work for a major organization, have you ensured that 'ambassadors' are appointed within the different company institutions so as to ensure that local managers feel strongly involved in the initiative?			

Chapter 10: Pinpoint the target

Hunt down mistaken priorities	Yes	More or less	No, not yet
Do you know the three company priorities that are the most important to you?			
Have you made plans in order to ensure that head office departments do not add further priorities to these priorities?			
Do you intend to halt projects so as to ensure that there is no increase in the number of priorities?			
You have to talk the talk and walk the walk	**Yes**	**More or less**	**No, not yet**
Have you made this subject a priority at your various meetings, particularly ones that you organize with people directly answerable to you?			
When you visit your people on the ground, do you make it a priority to ask them questions about this subject?			
Put a new deal in their hands	**Yes**	**More or less**	**No, not yet**
Have you planned how this subject will be taken into account, compared to other everyday issues?			
Have you planned exactly how this issue is going to affect the fixed and variable pay of your staff?			
Could the contribution of one of your people in this field have a positive or negative effect on their career development?			

Chapter 11: Compare progress

Stop ticking boxes: compare progress	Yes	More or less	No, not yet
Have you set simple, comprehensible measurement criteria?			
Have you identified other companies with which a comparison is possible and appropriate?			
Have you begun to compare progress between similar units within your company?			
If so, have you fully explained that you are going to publish monthly progress comparisons?			

Chapter 12: Make execution your trademark

Make doing nothing impossible	Yes	More or less	No, not yet
When one of your people last failed to meet their commitments, did you fulfil your responsibilities?			

Embody execution	Yes	More or less	No, not yet
At the beginning of each of your meetings, does everyone report on actions taken in pursuit of commitments made at the previous meeting?			
At the end of each of your meetings, does everyone make specific commitments?			
Do you respond to every e-mail or phone call about the main issue within half a day? Do you find time for any further meeting on this issue within a week?			

Stop relying on your memory	Yes	More or less	No, not yet
Are all the tasks that you need to complete collected on a small number of easily accessible lists?			
Do you immediately carry out any task taking less than two minutes?			
Are you fully aware of the tasks with which you are behind schedule?			
Radiate optimism	Yes	More or less	No, not yet
Do you show that you are absolutely convinced, under all circumstances, of your team's ability to influence the course of events?			
Do you systematically help your people to attribute failures to specific reasons and surmountable causes?			
Do you systematically help them to connect each success to a general, ongoing cause, which will yield further success in the future?			

References

Allen, David (2003) *Getting Things Done: The art of stress-free productivity*, Penguin Books, New York

Bossidy, Larry and Charan, Ram (2002) *Execution: The discipline of getting things done*, Crown Business, New York

Colvin, Geoff (2008) *Talent Is Overrated*, Portfolio, New York

Covey, Stephen R (1989) *The Seven Habits of Highly Effective People*, Free Press, New York

Descarpentries, Jean-Marie and Korda, Philippe (2007) *L'entreprise réconciliée*, Albin Michel, Paris

Ericsson, K Anders (ed) (1996) *The Road to Excellence*, Lawrence Erlbaum Associates, Mahwah, NJ

Frankl, Viktor (1984) *Man's Search for Meaning*, Washington Square Press, New York

Frisk, Bob (2008) When teams can't decide, *Harvard Business Review*, November

Gerstner, Lou (2004) *Who Says Elephants Can't Dance?*, Harper Business, New York

Gittell, Jody Hoffer (2003) *The Southwest Airlines Way*, McGraw-Hill, New York

Goleman, Daniel (1995) *Emotional Intelligence: Why it can matter more than IQ*, Bantam, New York

Heilman, ME and Stopeck, MH (1985) Attractiveness and corporate success, *Journal of Applied Psychology*, **70** (2), pp 379–88

Kaplan, Robert and Norton, David (2006) *Alignment: Using the balanced scorecard to create corporate synergies*, Harvard Business School Press, Boston, MA

Kirby, Julia and Stewart, Thomas A (2007) The institutional yes: an interview with Jeff Bezos, *Harvard Business Review*, October

Koestenbaum, Peter (2002) *Leadership: The inner side of greatness, a philosophy for leaders*, Jossey-Bass, San Francisco, CA

Kotter, John (1996) *Leading Change*, Harvard Business School Press, Boston, MA

Kotter, John (2008) *A Sense of Urgency*, Harvard Business School Press, Boston, MA

Loehr, Jim and Schwartz, Tony (2003) *The Power of Full Engagement*, Free Press, New York

Medina, John (2009) *Brain Rules*, Pear Press, Seattle, WA

Parker, James (2007) *Do the Right Thing*, Wharton School Publishing, Philadelphia, PA

Pascale, Richard Tanner and Sternin, Jerry (2005) Your company's secret change agents, *Harvard Business Review*, May

Robbins, Stephen P *et al* (2007) *Organisational Behaviour*, Pearson Education, Harlow

Schaffer, Robert H and Thomson, Harvey A (1992) Successful change programs begin with results, *Harvard Business Review*, January

Seligman, Martin P (2004) *Learned Optimism*, Free Press, New York

Stewart, Ian (2007) *Transactional Analysis Counselling in Action*, Sage, Newbury Park, CA

Further reading

Buckingham, Marcus and Clifton, Donald (2001) *Now, Discover Your Strengths*, Free Press, New York

Buckingham, Marcus and Coffman, Curt (1999) *First, Break All the Rules*, Simon & Schuster, New York

Carlzon, Jan (1989) *Moments of Truth*, Harper & Row, New York

Dupuy, François (1999) *The Customer's Victory: From corporation to cooperation*, Macmillan Business, London and Indiana University Press, Bloomington

Gilbert, Xavier, Büchel, Bettina and Davidson, Rhoda (2007) *Smarter Execution*, Financial Times Management, London

Kouzes, Jim and Posner, Barry (2008) *The Leadership Challenge*, 4th edn, Jossey-Bass, San Francisco, CA

Maister, David (2008) *Strategy and the Fat Smoker*, Spangle Press, Boston, MA

Pink, Daniel H (2006) *A Whole New Mind: Why right-brainers will rule the future*, Riverhead Books, New York

Wagner, Rodd and Harter, James K (2007) *12: The elements of great managing*, Gallup Press, New York

Index